You Can't
Take It
With You

Also by David C. Larsen

WHO GETS IT WHEN YOU GO?

David C. Larsen

You Can't Take It With You

*A Step-by-Step,
Personalized Approach to Your Will
to Avoid Probate and Estate Taxes*

Vintage Books
A Division of Random House
New York

A Vintage Original,
First Edition, March 1988

Copyright © 1988 by David C. Larsen
Illustrations copyright © 1988 by Phil Scheuer

LIBRARY OF CONGRESS CATALOGING-IN-PUBLICATION DATA
Larsen, David C., 1944–
    You Can't Take It With You
    1. Estate planning—United States—Popular works.
2. Inheritance and transfer tax—Law and legislation—
United States—Popular works. I. Title.
KF750.Z9L34   1988   343.7305'3   87-20965
ISBN 0-394-75543-X (pbk.)   347.30353

Text design by Mary A. Wirth

Manufactured in the United States of America
10 9 8 7 6 5 4

To my father and the memory of my mother

Foreword

We've all heard the rumors and stories: "The kids will have to sell the farm after we're gone in order to pay the taxes" or "How can the kids afford to inherit anything from us if they have to pay the probate and taxes?" or "Aunt Tillie's estate went through probate and it took five years and the fees ate up most of her estate."

Well, it ain't necessarily so.

There is no reason whatsoever for your heirs to pay any estate taxes when you die, or for your heirs to have to go through probate when you die. The purpose of this book is to explain to you, in uncomplicated, nonlegal language, how you can set up your affairs in such a way as to avoid estate taxes and probate when you die. It will take you through the process step by step and show you how you can get each one of your assets at your death to the person or persons you want, without causing any estate tax or probate.

The book, however, is not intended as a substitute for sound legal advice. You should definitely consult your lawyer before implementing any part of your will, trust, or estate plan. And incidentally, the examples of "wills" and "trusts" that are scattered throughout the book are all abbreviated "translations" in everyday English (and not in legalese!) of lengthier and more formal documents that your lawyer would draw up for you. Therefore, don't use any of these examples as forms, because they're not intended for that use at all; they're just meant to be illustrations of different approaches and techniques that might be useful to you.

In addition to giving you some information, the book may very well save you some money at the lawyer's office. Since most lawyers charge "by the hour" for their time in assisting you in your estate planning, the better prepared you are when you first walk into the lawyer's office, the less time you're going to take, which should translate into a smaller bill for you.

Ready? Here we go.

Contents

You Can't Take It With You

Chapter 1

Getting Oriented

This book will show you how to get your wealth to the people you want at your death, with no probate and no estate taxes. We will see that avoiding probate and avoiding estate taxes is relatively easy. In fact, it's mostly mechanical: You set up your will or trust in a certain way, put in certain provisions and words (and leave out others), and your heirs can inherit your estate without any probate and without any estate taxes. So, at the start, don't be too concerned with probate and estate taxes. While it's true that they can take a huge monetary bite out of your estate, meaning that your heirs receive less than you had when you died, they can both be avoided relatively easily, in perfectly honest and legal ways.

Instead, you should begin at the beginning by assessing your present wealth and defining your objectives. The way to do this is by asking, "What do I have to leave behind me if I should die tomorrow, and to whom would I like it left?" Once those questions are answered in your mind and you know where you are headed, then this book will show you how to attain your ends without getting caught in the clutter and expense of probate and estate taxes.

What Are You Worth?

The first step is to determine what assets you would have to leave if you were to pass away tomorrow. There is a checklist on page 8 that you should take a few minutes to fill out at this time. By spending a few minutes with this now, the rest of the book will be more meaningful to you, since you'll be able to see exactly how certain legal concepts apply to your own specific estate.

There are just three precautions you should observe in filling out the checklist. First, don't be concerned about the "might-be's," the assets you may have someday in the future, such as an inheritance from your parents, a summer home you might purchase, or a lottery you might win. Just put down what you have right now. Second, put down your assets at their present fair market value. Their cost to you is not important, so don't include it. Try to be honest when you put down the fair market value. The value you are looking for is what the asset would sell for today to an unrelated third party, assuming you didn't have to sell to raise the money quickly, and the buyer wasn't desperate to buy. Third, for the time being, just put down any co-owned assets in the third column. You'll learn later that there are three distinct types of co-ownership, each with its own distinct rules and regulations.

To help you along in the completion of your own personal checklist, and also to give some models that we'll use later on in explaining some probate and tax rules, there are two sample checklists on pages 6 and 7, one for a single person and one for a married couple.

Who Should Get Your Wealth?

Okay, now that your checklist is filled in, you know where you stand today, and you know what you would have to give away if you were to die tomorrow. The next questions are to determine how you want to handle this wealth while you're living, and to whom you would like to give it at your death. If you are like many people, your objectives might be as follows:

1. Keep control, ownership, and benefits of all your assets as long as you are alive. In other words: "I made it, I'll keep it as long as I can."

2. If you should become incapacitated, either mentally or physically, someone should step in immediately to deal with your financial affairs, without the hassles of getting lawyers or a court involved.

3. At your death, if you are married, all of your wealth would go to your surviving spouse. (You might check to see if your spouse will do likewise!)

4. At the death of the surviving spouse (if you're married), or at your death (if you're single), then all of your

CHECKLIST FOR SALLY SINGLE

ASSETS (CURRENT MARKET VALUE)	OWNED BY HUSBAND	OWNED BY WIFE	CO-OWNERSHIP	TOTAL
Life Insurance (Face Value)		$ 75,000		$ 75,000
Cash (Checking, Savings, etc.)		35,000		35,000
Money Market Certificates, Certificates of Deposit		20,000		20,000
IRA, Profit Sharing, Pension, HR-10		18,000		18,000
Stocks & Bonds		8,000		8,000
Real Estate—Residence		150,000		150,000
—Vacation/ Rental		—		—
Money Due You (Notes)		—		—
Deferred Compensation		—		—
Sole Proprietorship or Partnership Interest		—		—
Miscellaneous Property (Auto, Furniture, Jewelry, Antiques, Art, etc.)		24,000		24,000
TOTAL ASSETS		$330,000		$330,000
LIABILITIES Mortgages		$ 25,000		$ 25,000
Notes & Other Loans		5,000		5,000
TOTAL LIABILITIES		$ 30,000		$ 30,000
NET ESTATE		$300,000		$300,000

CHECKLIST FOR MIKE AND MINERVA MARRIED

ASSETS (CURRENT MARKET VALUE)	OWNED BY HUSBAND	OWNED BY WIFE	CO-OWNERSHIP	TOTAL
Life Insurance (Face Value)	$145,000	$ 75,000		$ 220,000
Cash (Checking, Savings, etc.)	15,000	12,000	20,000	47,000
Money Market Certificates, Certificates of Deposit			125,000	125,000
IRA, Profit Sharing, Pension, HR-10	78,000	54,000		132,000
Stocks & Bonds			56,000	56,000
Real Estate—Residence			220,000	220,000
—Vacation/ Rental			95,000	95,000
Money Due You (Notes)				—
Deferred Compensation				—
Sole Proprietorship or Partnership Interest		112,000		112,000
Miscellaneous Property (Auto, Furniture, Jewelry, Antiques, Art, etc.)	11,000	46,000	32,000	89,000
TOTAL ASSETS	$249,000	$299,000	$548,000	$1,096,000
LIABILITIES Mortgages			$106,000	$ 106,000
Notes & Other Loans	45,000	30,000	15,000	90,000
TOTAL LIABILITIES	$ 45,000	$ 30,000	$121,000	$ 196,000
NET ESTATE	$204,000	$269,000	$427,000	$ 900,000

CHECKLIST FOR THE READER

ASSETS (CURRENT MARKET VALUE)	OWNED BY HUSBAND	OWNED BY WIFE	CO-OWNERSHIP	TOTAL
Life Insurance (Face Value)				
Cash (Checking, Savings, etc.)				
Money Market Certificates, Certificates of Deposit				
IRA, Profit Sharing, Pension, HR-10				
Stocks & Bonds				
Real Estate—Residence				
—Vacation/ Rental				
Money Due You (Notes)				
Deferred Compensation				
Sole Proprietorship or Partnership Interest				
Miscellaneous Property (Auto, Furniture, Jewelry, Antiques, Art, etc.)				
TOTAL ASSETS				

LIABILITIES				
Mortgages				
Notes & Other Loans				
TOTAL LIABILITIES				

NET ESTATE				

wealth would go to your children. (You might begin thinking about whether they should receive equal or unequal shares, and whether they should receive their shares at different ages.)

5. If you don't have any children, then you might like your wealth to go to your brothers, sisters, parents, nieces, nephews, a charity, your alma mater, or so on. What fractional share or asset should each receive?

6. When your wealth is transmitted from you to your heirs, you would like to avoid probate expense and delay, and you would like to avoid estate taxes.

Let's take these fairly common objectives, flesh them out a bit, and maybe give you a few ideas. For example, here is a more complete scenario for a married couple with two children. As their objectives, they would like full ownership and control of all their assets while they are living. When one of them dies, they would like the surviving spouse to inherit all of the wealth. After the surviving spouse dies, they would like all of their wealth to go to the two children in equal shares. Thus far, this is hardly an unusual approach for a married couple with children, so let's add a wrinkle. Let's assume that the children are quite young, below the age of majority (eighteen in most states). Therefore, while the parents want the two children to inherit all their wealth after both parents have died, for the next few years they wouldn't want their children to receive the wealth outright. Instead, they would like to postpone the date at which each child receives his or her half share until each child has reached a more mature age, for example (and there is nothing magic about this age), age thirty. Until each child reaches age thirty, the parents would like the child's half share to be available to the child for the child's education, food, clothing, housing, travel, and health needs. They would like somebody to be in charge of the child's half share, and to make these distributions to the child as the child is growing up.

What the parents really would like here, although they may not know it by this name, is a *trust* for their children. A trust is an arrangement in which somebody (a *trustee*) holds some or all of your assets, invests them, and uses the income (and principal, if need be) to pay out to someone else (the *beneficiaries*—here, the children). The parents (who are the owners of the wealth) set up all the rules for the trust: who the trustee will be; the type of investments the trustee can make; how much or how little the trustee should distribute to the children; for what purposes distributions may be made to the children (education? health needs? food? clothing? housing? travel? a new car?); whether a distribution of a certain amount of money to one child would require an equal distribution of the same amount of money to the other child; and at what age the trust arrangement should end and each child receive the balance of his or her share.

Trusts are the key to avoiding probate and saving estate taxes, so we will definitely look at them in much greater detail throughout the book.

Now let's shift and look at a single person. A fleshed-out set of objectives for a single person might be something like this: During her life, the single person would like to retain full control and ownership of all her assets. If she becomes incapacitated, she would like someone to manage her financial affairs for her. At her death, if she had children, she could certainly have objectives for them very similar to the ones discussed above for the married couple with children. If she does not have children (or even if she does but doesn't want to leave the little monsters anything), she might want to leave her estate to her parents, or to her brothers and sisters. But rather than leave her estate outright to them, she might consider putting it into a trust for their use and benefit for the remainder of their lives. This is because there can be problems with an outright transfer of wealth to her parents or brothers and sisters. First, if she gives a share of her estate to her brother, for example, then at her death her brother will become the owner of that share, and can do with it as he likes. This means that he can either give it away during his lifetime or transfer it under his will at his death to someone that our single person doesn't like (for example, an evil nephew). Second, any asset that our single person leaves outright to her brother will be included in his taxable estate when he passes away later on, thereby potentially increasing his estate taxes.

On the other hand, if our single person were to leave an asset in trust for her brother, these problems would not occur. For example, let's assume she wants her brother to get her house when she dies. If she simply leaves it to him in her will, with no strings attached (and no trust, either), then once she dies and he gets it, he can do with it as he likes. Alternatively, she could establish a trust that would hold her house for her brother for the rest of his life. She could include (if she wanted) these provisions in her trust: Her brother could be the trustee; he (and his family) could use the house rent-free; they could rent it out and pocket the rentals; or the house could be sold, the money invested, and the interest paid to her brother. Upon his death, her trust would provide that the house (or, if it was sold, the money) would go to a specific niece or nephew, whom our single person would name right in the trust document, rather than being available for the brother to give to whomever he wants. Also, if the trust is set up the right way with the proper provisions (which we'll learn about), it will not be subject to estate taxes when the brother dies, even though he has had use and control of the house and the trust during his lifetime.

With a trust, then, our single person could (1) benefit the brother that she wants to benefit; (2) keep the asset out of the hands of people she doesn't like; (3) direct where the house is going to go after the brother has died; and (4) keep the house from being taxed when her brother passes away.

Bridging the Gap

Now that you have filled out your checklist and have a fairly good idea of the wealth that you would have to leave if you were to die, and now that you have thought through your objectives in a preliminary kind of way, the next step is to see what means are available to you to attain your objectives. In other words, how do you get your wealth from "here" to "there"? You are probably thinking that the best way to attain your objectives is through a will. Good! A will is the traditional and best starting point for attaining your objectives, but, as we will soon see, it may not provide all the answers. Nevertheless, let's spend a little time and see what a will can do for you.

Chapter 2

The Role of the Will

A will really is a starting point, a building block, a foundation. It may not (as we will soon see) be the answer to each and every one of the objectives that you have set out for yourself. However, no estate plan is complete without a will.

Let's have a look at a simple will for Sally Single, just so you can see how painless a will can be.

• • •

Will

I leave everything I have to my brother, Sam.

/s/ Sally Single

We witnessed Sally sign after she told us this was her will.

_____ /s/ Tom Witness

_____ /s/ Velma Witness

_____ /s/ Harry Witness

Let's see just what Sally has here. It seems pretty simple: At her death, she's leaving "everything she has" to her brother, Sam. Well, get ready for the first surprise of the book (or maybe just this chapter): Sally's will is not going to control every asset she has, and Sam may not in fact get everything Sally owns. Why not? Well, because there are certain things she could own that a will has no power to direct. The law divides your various assets into two separate groups: those assets that your will does not control, and those assets that your will does control. Let's take these two separate groups one at a time. You'll see that it may take more than a will to get your assets going in the right direction; it takes some thought, care, and coordination.

Your Will Does Not Control These Assets

There are four categories of assets that your will does not control: (1) your life insurance; (2) your retirement proceeds; (3) any asset held as joint tenants with rights of survivorship with another party; and (4) any asset held as tenants by the entirety with your spouse.

Life insurance

Life insurance proceeds are not payable in accordance with your will's provisions. Instead, you fill out a beneficiary designation form, which your insurance company will supply you with, and at your death the life insurance proceeds will be paid to the beneficiary you have named. Whether you have a will or not is immaterial: Your life insurance proceeds will be paid to the beneficiary you have named in the policy or in the form. In fact, even if your will purports to name who the beneficiary of a life insurance policy should be, or even if your will says "I want my life insurance proceeds to be paid to Joe," your will would not control the proceeds.

There are two slight exceptions to this. If you have your life insurance beneficiary designated as "my estate," or if all of your named beneficiaries die before you do, then the life insurance company will pay your life insurance monies to your estate, which your will does control. But naming your estate as the beneficiary of your policy is not a very wise thing to do. The reason is that the proceeds would then have to go through probate, and during the course of probate (as we'll see a little later), the proceeds would be subject to any claims of creditors that you might have. In addition, the proceeds would increase the value of your probate estate, thereby increasing the fees payable to your executor and also to the executor's lawyer, if there is one involved in your probate proceedings. Therefore, most people do not name their estate as a beneficiary of their policy, but instead have it payable directly to some personal beneficiary, and take the extra precaution of naming a "secondary" or "contingent" beneficiary who would receive the proceeds if the "primary" benficiary dies before, or at the same time as, the insured person.

Your retirement plan proceeds

If you have an IRA (individual retirement account), a pension plan, profit-sharing plan, Keogh/HR-10, or any other kind of retirement plan or annuity, you probably have the opportunity to name a beneficiary who would receive the plan benefits if you were to die before all the benefits were paid to you. Again, these benefits would be paid to your named beneficiary, whom you have designated on appropriate forms given to you by your employer or bank or trust company. These proceeds would not be payable under the provisions of your will, so in this regard they are similar to your life insurance proceeds. Also, like life insurance proceeds, if all of your named beneficiaries have died before you die, or if you have named "my estate" as the beneficiary of your retirment proceeds, then the retirement monies would be paid to your estate, which your will does control.

Joint tenancy with rights of survivorship

Two or more people, as you well know, can own an asset together. "A" and "B" can own a car together; "C," "D," "E," and "F" can own a condominium (or a bank account, or a stock, etc.) together. There are three different legal ways co-owners can own an asset together. One of these ways is called *joint tenants with rights of survivorship*, sometimes abbreviated as *joint tenants* or sometimes as *JTWROS*. (By the way, the word *tenant* just means "owner.") This type of ownership means that if one of the co-owners dies, his or her share of the asset *automatically* goes to the surviving co-owner(s). It augments their shares. The deceased co-owner's share is not distributable under the deceased's will. For example, if three people own a condominium apartment as joint tenants with rights of survivorship, and one of them dies, his one-third share of that condominium apartment would not be disposable under his will, but instead would automatically go to the two surviving co-owners. The two co-owners would then each own one half of the condominium apartment instead of one third.

As you can see, joint tenancy has to be thought through very carefully. Since the deceased's will has no control whatsoever over his share of a joint tenancy asset, the deceased co-owner's family could be very disappointed when the deceased's share of the asset does not go to them, but instead goes to the surviving joint tenants. If a joint tenant wishes to have control over his or her separate share, what he or she wants is not a joint tenancy but instead a *tenancy in common* (see below).

How can you tell whether a particular asset you co-own with another person is joint tenants with rights of survivorship? If the asset is a piece of real estate, you can look at the deed. If it is a stock, you can look at the face of the stock certificate. If it is a bank account, you can check with an officer at the bank. If you have any confusion regarding this at all, simply check with the appropriate institution (bank, stock brokerage house, escrow company, mortgage company, etc.).

Many people ask whether a co-owned bank account is a joint tenancy if certain words are used to separate the owners. For example, is there any difference between "John and Mary," "John or Mary," "John and/or Mary," or "John–

Mary"? The answer to this depends upon the bank's own rules, so you should give them a call and ask them whether your co-owned bank account is a joint tenancy. If it is, and you don't want one, then just read on.

Tenancy by the entirety

This is the second of the three ways of co-ownership. It's a form of co-ownership between husband and wife that provides that when the first of them dies, the survivor automatically receives the entire asset. In other words, it is exactly like a joint tenancy with rights of survivorship, but it can only be between a husband and a wife. You cannot have a tenancy by the entirety between a father and son, mother and daughter, or anyone else other than a husband and wife. Some states allow a tenancy by the entirety only for real estate; other states allow a tenancy by the entirety for real estate and also bank accounts, stocks, automobiles, and any other kind of registered asset. A major advantage in some states to an asset owned as tenants by the entirety is this: If one of the spouses were to get sued and is found liable (for example, in a car crash), and didn't have adequate insurance protection to completely discharge the judgment against him or her, then the creditor would go after the assets the spouse owned in order to collect. However, any asset that the spouse owned as a tenant by the entirety with his or her spouse would not be subject to the creditor's claims. Notice, however, that this form of co-ownership would not prevent a creditor from taking the asset if he were to sue *both* husband and wife and receive a judgment against them both.

In summary, then, there are four categories of assets your will won't control: (1) life insurance; (2) retirement plan proceeds; (3) any asset owned as joint tenants with another person or persons; and (4) any asset owned as tenancy by the entirety. What is left for your will to control?

Assets That Are Controlled by Your Will

There are two categories of assets that your will *does* control.

Your co-ownership as a tenant in common

The third and final way of co-owning an asset with one or more other parties is called *tenancy in common*. Under this form of co-ownership, each co-owner has a distinct and divisible share of the asset that he or she can leave under his or her will. The deceased co-owner's share will not go to the other co-owners unless the deceased co-owner happens to leave it to them under his or her will.

EXAMPLE: John, Mary, and Rachel own a condominium apartment together. They deliberately took title to the property on the deed as tenants in common rather than as joint tenants with rights of survivorship, because each of them wishes to leave his or her share under his or her will at death. When Rachel, for example, dies, she can leave her share to whomever she wants under her will, and then John and Mary will have that person as a new co-owner with them. Incidentally, it is perfectly possible for people to own unequal shares as tenants in common: They should just make sure that the deed, which establishes their title and ownership to the apartment, recites that they are unequal owners, and shows the correct and proper percentage of ownership of each.

Solely owned assets

Any asset that you own by yourself, without any form of co-ownership, is controlled by, and disposable by, your will. For example, if you own a bank account in your name, a stock in your name, a house in your name, or any other asset that is *yours alone*, that asset is controlled by your will. If you do not have a will, then your state will "write a will for you" and will, at your death, distribute the asset to the persons on your family tree (more on this shortly).

Here's a sidelight for those residents of the nine "community property" states (Arizona, California, Idaho, Louisiana, Nevada, New Mexico, Texas, Washington, and Wisconsin). If you're married and a resident of one of those states, then 50 percent of any money you earn at your job and any assets you buy with that money belong to your spouse. You may keep the money yourself, or take title to the asset in your name alone, but the community property law says that one half of that money or asset belongs to your spouse, and your will won't control it.

EXAMPLE: Jim and Mary are married and reside in a community property state. Jim earns $20,000 at his job. He deposits $6,000 in a joint tenancy bank account with Mary, $8,000 in a stock brokerage account in his own name, and buys a $6,000 diamond ring for himself. At his death, the bank account goes to Mary (because it was joint tenancy), one half of the stock account and ring belong to Mary under the community property laws, and the other half is disposable under Jim's will. Notice that Jim's will can't dispose of *all* the stock account and ring simply because, under the community property law, he didn't own all of them; he only owned 50 percent.

Summary

There are, therefore, six different categories into which the law segregates your various assets: (1) life insurance; (2) retirement plans; (3) solely owned assets; and then the co-owned assets: (4) joint tenants with rights of survivorship; (5) tenants by the entirety; and (6) tenants in common. Every asset you own, from your toaster to your television to your home, can be put into one of these six categories, and that simplifies things greatly: If you want to know where a particular asset goes at your death, just fit it into its proper category and use the rules for that category discussed above. Don't get caught up in the impossible task of asking, "Where does my ring go? Where does my TV go? my car? home? savings and loan account? bond? gun? dog?" The law couldn't and doesn't treat each of these things with separate rules for the specific item, and neither should you. Just fit each into one of the six categories; the rules for each are easy enough.

If you would take a minute or two to look back at your own personal checklist, which you should have completed by now, it would be helpful at this point for you to determine into which of the three categories your co-owned assets fall (joint tenancy, tenancy by the entirety, or tenancy in common). From this point forward, we will be talking very specifically about the distinct types of co-ownership, so it's a good idea to get your own personal checklist in order now. And while you're looking at your checklist, you should think through whether you have your six categories of assets going to the right people. Because any will you might have will only control two of the six categories, you can appreciate the need for some thought and coordination regarding the other four categories. For example, many people are surprised to learn that a co-ownership might be a joint tenancy, meaning that when they die, the other co-owner would receive the entire asset. If this is not what you want, then you should change the joint ownership from a joint tenancy to a tenancy in common or, if your co-owner agrees with this, simply take back the asset yourself so that it will be part of your solely owned assets. (If your co-owner releases all his or her share to you, there may be a gift tax involved. See Chapter 5.) You should also look to see that your beneficiary designations on your life insurance and retirement funds are up to date. It's not at all uncommon for a married couple to purchase a life insurance policy early in the marriage, before they have all of their children, and to name one child as contingent beneficiary. Later on, when they have more children, the beneficiary designation should be changed to include *all* the children, but somehow people seem to forget about this.

One final comment before we look at several wills. Across America, most married couples own their assets jointly, as joint tenants with rights of survivorship, or as tenants by the entirety. As we have seen, when the first spouse dies, all of the assets held in joint tenancy or as tenants by the entirety will automatically, without a will, go to the surviving spouse. Therefore, many married couples feel there is no need for a will. This is asking for trouble! It is true that after one spouse dies, no will is needed to get the joint tenancy assets or tenancy by the entirety assets to the surviving spouse; that happens automatically, without a will. Take note, however, that the instant after the first spouse has died, the surviving spouse receives those assets, and then those assets are owned by the surviving spouse in his or her sole name. In other words, those assets have jumped from joint tenancy or tenancy by the entirety to assets that are solely held by the surviving spouse. And it is precisely those solely held assets that are subject to a person's will; those are the assets the surviving spouse needs a will to direct. Without a will, state laws take over and the assets get scattered to people on your family tree. Therefore, since a married couple never knows which spouse is going to die first and which second, they should make sure that each spouse has a will. While it's true that the first will is "wasted" in that it would not affect any jointly held or tenancy by the entirety asset, it is also true that the surviving spouse unquestionably must have a will in order to direct the assets that were formerly jointly held with the deceased spouse.

A Simple Will

Let's have a look at a simple will for Sally Single that's more complete than the earlier one that was one sentence long. A *simple will*, by the way, is a will that leaves one's estate outright to one or more people or institutions, and does not establish a trust. If you'll look back on page 6, you will see the assets that Sally owns. You will note that all of her assets, except for her life insurance and retirement plan, are going to be controlled by her will; she has no co-owned assets at all. This will, therefore, is going to control $207,000 of her assets (i.e., her net estate of $300,000 less her life insurance [$75,000] and retirement [$18,000]). She has to take special care to be sure that the beneficiary on her life insurance and retirement plan is exactly the person that she wants.

Last Will and Testament of Sally Single

I, Sally Single, a resident of the State of _____ , hereby make my last will and testament:

1. I hereby revoke all prior wills and codicils I have made.
2. I am presently single, and have no children or other descendants.
3. I give all my jewelry to my niece, NORMA SINGLE, if she survives me.
4. I give the sum of $20,000 to my brother, SAM SINGLE, if he survives me, and if he does not survive me, then to NORMA SINGLE, if she survives me.
5. I give all my stocks and bonds to the American Red Cross, Nevada Chapter.
6. I give all the remainder of my assets in the following shares: 25% to SAM SINGLE, 35% to my sister, PAMELA WILKINSON, 25% to my friend, JOHN LANG, and 15% to his wife, EVELYN LANG. The share of any of such persons who does not survive me shall be divided among the remaining shares, pro rata.
7. I authorize my executor, if money has to be raised to pay my debts, taxes, or probate fees, to sell any assets I may own.

8. I name SAM SINGLE to serve as my executor, without bond. If he for any reason fails to serve, then I name EVELYN LANG as executor, also without bond.

Dated: _____ /s/ Sally Single

    On _____ , Sally Single told us this was her will and asked us to witness her signature. We all were together and saw her sign her will; we believe she is over the age of majority and of sound mind.

_____ /s/ <u>Wilma Witness</u>

_____ /s/ <u>Walter Witness</u>

_____ /s/ <u>Webley Witness</u>

Dying Without a Will

You can see the thought and precision with which Sally has divided up her estate. Specific items and amounts are going to specific people—that's the real purpose of a will. But what would have happened had Sally said, "Forget about a will for me—let 'em fight it out"? Well, Sally would have lots of company in this kind of thinking since 70 percent of Americans die without wills, but it's not choice company to be in. It's odd that this many people die without wills. Most of us take precautions against calamities that *may* happen (we take an umbrella to work, we insure our homes and cars), but a huge number of us take no care against the calamity that is *certain* to happen. Because so many die without wills, let's take a few minutes to see what's going to happen at their death (and also, if you're getting discouraged, to revive your flagging spirits!).

Dying without a will (or *intestate*) leaves a real mess for your family, since two of the six categories will have no specific direction to go in (the other four categories are unaffected). Your solely owned assets and your share as a tenant in common have no specifically designated recipient, since you left no will. Does the state take your assets in those two categories? Probably not. Each state has its own separate laws that, for a resident who dies without a will, provide to whom those assets go.* The results can be quite surprising. Some of those assets (a modest flat dollar amount in some states, one third in some states, one half in other states, but rarely all) could go to your spouse; some of those assets could go to your children; some of those assets could go to your parents, your brothers, sisters, nieces, nephews, and so on. Who gets what really depends upon who is on your family tree at the time you die. The closer they are on the family tree to you, the more they get. The biggest surprise, and disappointment, is that in most states your spouse will not receive everything you had in those two categories when you died. This is quite contrary to what most married couples want. Furthermore, in most states your children, assuming they get anything at all, will share whatever they get equally. Again, this may not be fair or what you wanted. For example, if you have paid for the education of one child all the way through college, but an-

* If you're really interested in exactly where your assets go if you die without a will (or *intestate*), see Chapter 1 of *Who Gets It When You Go?* (Random House, 1982).

other child is just starting out in college, is it really fair that, if you should die without a will, both children would receive equal amounts of your estate? Most people would probably think not. However, if you don't write a will, you don't have any control as to where your two categories go. Your state's laws will control this, and you can leave behind you a wreckage of hopes and expectations.

Besides being unable to direct who gets what, what are some other difficulties of dying without a will?

Naming a guardian and making a trust for minor children

For parents with minor children, not having a will can create a very difficult family situation. This is because another role of a will is to name a guardian for any minor children you might have. If both parents die, the guardian's job is to become the child's surrogate parent, to take the child into the guardian's home and to raise the child as one of the guardian's own. Without a will, the probate judge will simply name somebody in your family or in your spouse's family to raise and educate your child until the child reaches the age of majority. It's entirely possible that a completely unsuitable person would be chosen by the probate judge. The best way to prevent this kind of thing from happening is to write a will and specify your child's guardian.

Another problem for parents of minor children is that, without a will, each child will inherit his or her share of the estate when the child reaches the age of majority. The age of majority in most states is eighteen. Most parents, if they thought about it, would agree that age eighteen is entirely too young for a child to receive any substantial inheritance at all. Indeed, a large inheritance at that age could ruin a child's motivations for college, or for any kind of hard work. To avoid this early inheritance, a parent can establish a trust in the parent's will. The trust would hold a share of the parent's estate for the child until the child attained a more mature age (for example, twenty-eight) and could in the meantime, if the parent wished, make partial distributions for education, health needs, food, clothing, housing, and so on.

Naming your executor

Another major role of a will is that of naming your executor and waiving bond for your executor. (A *bond* is a form of insurance that your estate has to pay for unless you waive its necessity in your will.) The *executor* is the person who, after your death, collects, preserves, and safeguards your assets, pays your debts, pays your income and estate taxes, and distributes your assets in accordance with your will, or if you have no will, then in accordance with your state's laws. Clearly, the executor is a very important person for your wealth and also for your family, since he or she will be closely involved with them for some time. A choice of a poor executor can mean extra headaches for your family after you are gone. And if you have no will, you cannot have named an executor. The probate judge will simply find somebody and name him or her as your executor, and your family and heirs can only hope that the best will be done. Would you really want your spendthrift brother to be your executor? If not, then you ought to think about writing a will and naming your own executor.

· · ·

Funeral, burial, organ donations
A will is the traditional and appropriate place to specify your funeral and burial wishes. You can also use your will to donate your organs.*

Probate and estate taxes
Both these hobgoblins can be avoided, but not without careful planning. If you die without a will, they are going to be the worst they can be for your situation.

Making Your Own Will

Well, none of these intestate problems is going to plague Sally, because she's in the well-prepared 30 percent of us who have wills.

Can you make your own will? Sure. You can also do your own lobotomy, and the results are likely to be the same. Having a lawyer is advisable in drawing up a will for a number of reasons. First, an attorney has greater experience than Sally in the area of wills, trusts, probate, and estate taxes, and can suggest many options to her that she may never have considered. Second, if a will's provisions are not drawn up precisely and clearly, there's going to be confusion after Sally dies and the will is shown to those affected by it. Third, as we'll soon see, avoiding probate and estate taxes needs special training and expertise, and

---

* If you decide to donate your organs, be sure to contact the institution that will receive them (for example, the Lions' Eye Bank, your local university, etc.) so it can supply you with an "organ donor" card or identification to keep in your wallet or purse to ensure immediate care of the organs upon your death.

if you forget or include a seemingly insignificant word or two, it can have an enormous impact on your probate or estate taxes. Finally, many wills are contested over whether the deceased had the requisite mental capacity to make a will, or whether the will was signed by the deceased and witnesses in the proper way. A lawyer, being trained to recognize these problems, can take precautions to prevent them from destroying your will. The bottom line is that drawing up a will is, like plumbing or brain surgery, a specialty that takes a trained specialist, and if you're going to have a will at all, you ought to have a proper and correct one.

A Testamentary Trust

Now let's look at another will that Sally might have her lawyer write for her, one that establishes a trust. The kind of trust that is established in a person's will is called a *testamentary trust*, because it appears in a person's last will and testament. This kind of a trust does *not* avoid probate. We will see later on that only a living trust will avoid probate.

Again, all Sally's assets except her life insurance and retirement plan will be distributed under this will's provisions. This will, then, controls $207,000 worth of her assets.

Last Will and Testament of Sally Single

I, Sally Single, a resident of _____ , hereby make my last will and testament:
1. I hereby revoke all wills and codicils which have been executed by me earlier.
2. I am single, and have no children or other descendants.

3. I direct that my eyes be donated to the Lions Eye Bank, that my body be cremated, and the ashes scattered at sea.

4. I give my jewelry, clothing, and personal effects to PAMELA WILKINSON, if she survives me.

5. I give all of my furniture, furnishings, and other tangible personal property located in my residence (other than items given in ¶ 4) to PAMELA WILKINSON and LINDA OLSEN, to divide between them as they see fit, or if they cannot agree, then as my executor shall decide in its sole discretion.

6. I give all the rest of my assets to LARRY LEDGER, as trustee, to hold in trust under the following provisions:

   (1) I wish my trustee to make investments with my trust assets, in his sole discretion. Therefore, he can sell my assets and buy new ones, or invest my money, in any way he sees fit.

   (2) All income and dividends and interest that the trustee earns shall be paid at least semiannually to my brother, SAM SINGLE, and my sister, PAMELA WILKINSON, equally, and after one dies, all to the other of them.

   (3) The comfort, care, and well-being of my said brother and sister are my main objectives in this trust. Therefore, I authorize the trustee to distribute principal to SAM and PAMELA, if, in the trustee's sole discretion, they, or either of them, should need principal for any of the following purposes: health care, food, clothing, housing, education, care, and comfort. The trustee can make unequal distribu-

tions to SAM and PAMELA. If the need exists, all the trust could be distributed to one person and not the other. There is no dollar limitation on the amount of principal that the trustee can distribute. In making any distributions of principal, my trustee shall first determine what other sources of income are available to SAM and PAMELA that might fulfill their needs, and, if such needs are fulfilled, then my trustee shall not make distributions of principal from this trust to them.

(4) This trust shall terminate after SAM and PAMELA have both died. When they have both died, whatever assets are then remaining in the trust, including any accumulated and accrued but undistributed income, shall be distributed to the following people in the following percentages: JOHN SINGLE, 50%; LEILANI WILKINSON, 30%; and LINDA OLSEN, 20%. If any of such persons is deceased at trust termination, his or her percentage share shall be distributed to his or her descendants, per stirpes,* or if none are alive, then to the remaining two named

---

* The phrase *descendants, per stirpes* is frequently used in wills and trusts because it's what many people want. It means that if a person is deceased, his or her share of your estate goes equally to his or her children, with the children of a deceased child taking the share their parent would have taken were such parent alive. For example, if John Single is deceased when the trust ends, his 50% goes equally to his four children, 12½% each. If one child is then deceased, his 12½% goes to his two children (John's grandchildren), 6¼% each, but if he were to have no children, then the child's 12½% would be divided equally among John's three remaining children.

        persons, pro rata according to their
        stated shares.

7. If LARRY LEDGER for any reason ceases to act as trustee, then I appoint ABC TRUST COMPANY to take over as trustee immediately. My trustee shall serve without bond.

8. I authorize my executor to sell any real estate, or any of my personal property, during the course of probate if such is necessary to pay my taxes, debts, or probate fees.

9. I appoint ABC TRUST COMPANY as my executor, to serve without bond.

Dated: _____ /s/ <u>Sally Single</u>

On _____ , Sally Single told us this was her will and asked us to witness her signature. We all were together and saw her sign her will; we believe she is over the age of majority and of sound mind.

_____ /s/ <u>Wilma Witness</u>

_____ /s/ <u>Walter Witness</u>

_____ /s/ <u>Webley Witness</u>

There is a difference between an executor and a trustee. The executor is the person or institution who probates your estate. After the lengthy process of probate is completed, the executor turns over your assets to the trustee, who then administers the trust in accordance with your written instructions. After turning over your estate, the executor's job is finished, and he, she, or it has nothing further to do with your estate or beneficiaries, and it's all up to the trustee to carry out your instructions.

Why did Sally Single decide to establish a testamentary trust for Sam and Pamela? She could, just as well, have created a will that would have given Sam and Pamela a share of her estate, outright, just as she did in ¶ 6 of her will on page 24. However, Sally is concerned about two things if she were to give Sam and Pamela a share outright. First, she's not at all convinced that either of them could manage the money that they might receive from her. She has seen them run through money before, and she doesn't believe that they would be any different with her money than they have been with their own money. Many trusts are established for heirs because of their inability to handle money wisely. When an heir is a minor, mentally disabled, or an adult with no "money sense," a trust is much better than an outright gift.

Second, and perhaps even more important to Sally, she believes that if she should give either of them a share outright, they would then turn around and either give that share to people Sally doesn't like, or will it to them under their wills at their death. In particular, Sally doesn't like Sam's spouse, and she doesn't like two of Pamela's children.

Nevertheless, Sally *does* want to provide for the well-being of Sam and Pamela. Is there any way that she can attain this objective but bypass the two problems (management and distribution to people she doesn't like) that we discussed above? The answer is that a testamentary trust would fit Sally's needs exactly. By reading her testamentary trust, you can see that it would provide for Sam and Pamela during their lives; Larry Ledger will professionally and competently manage the assets that Sally leaves; and after Sam and Pamela are deceased and no longer have any need of Sally's assistance, her testamentary trust would give the balance of her assets (whatever Sam and Pamela have not used) to people *Sally* wants, not people Sam and Pamela might want.

The provisions of the testamentary trust, above, are entirely illustrative, and are not mandatory. Sally can decide on any kinds of provisions she may want for her trust. Since it's her money, the law allows her to put whatever restrictions on it she may want, as long as such restrictions are not against public policy or do not require the commission of a crime. For example, she could have restricted the trustee's ability to invest, i.e., "Only invest in triple-A-rated bonds," or "Only invest in stocks from companies that are located in Iowa." However, because the market for good investments can swing from bonds to stocks to money market certificates to mortgages to real estate to gold and back again, and since her trust is going to be around for quite a few more years, Sally was well advised by her lawyer to give her trustee discretion in making whatever investments the trustee thought would give the best yield and protect Sally's assets in the best possible way. After all, Sally figures, if she can't trust her trustee to make the right decisions, who can she trust?

In addition, Sally could have restricted, had she wished, the income and principal distributions of her trust. Again, since it's her wealth and her will, she can be as strict or liberal as she likes. She could have, if she had wished, made the following restrictions: "Only $1,000 of income per year shall be distributed to each of Sam and Pamela, and distributions of principal to them shall be made only for medical emergencies." However, because Sally's objective is to provide for the welfare and well-being of Sam and Pamela, this kind of inflexible and restrictive standard might not accomplish her goal. Therefore, she has, again, left it pretty much up to the trustee's discretion with respect to principal distributions. If you reread her trust's provisions regarding principal distributions, you can see that she has placed a great deal of faith in her trustee to make the proper decisions after she is gone. But again, if you can't trust your trustee. . . .

Another Testamentary Trust

Now let's look at our married couple whose checklist appears on page 7 and see what kind of a will these people might require. Incidentally, Mike and Minerva checked on all their co-owned assets, and found, as they hoped and expected, that all such assets were held in either joint tenancy or tenancy by the entirety, and none was held in tenancy in common. If you look at their checklist, you can see that, upon the death of the first of the two spouses, very few assets are going to be under the control of that spouse's will. Like most couples, they have substantial amounts of life insurance, retirement monies, and assets held as joint tenants with rights of survivorship or as tenants by the entirety. None of those four categories of assets is going to be controlled by the will of the person who dies first. Nevertheless, as discussed above, it is very important that both husband and wife have wills, because even though the first will will be largely "wasted," the will of the survivor of them will be critical. Again, this is because after the first spouse dies, all of the assets held in joint tenancy with rights of survivorship and tenancy by the entirety shift over to the sole ownership of the surviving spouse. Also, the surviving spouse will likely be made the primary beneficiary on the deceased spouse's life insurance and retirement monies. The surviving spouse, therefore, will have substantial assets in her or his name alone, which are the assets that a will controls.

Our married couple met with their lawyer, and after a short conference, they decided upon the following. Their objectives are as follows: When one spouse dies, all assets should belong to the surviving spouse. When the surviving spouse dies, because the two children are minors, they do not want assets distributed to their children immediately. Instead, they would like the distribution postponed until the children reach a more mature age (they have selected age thirty-three). Until that time, they would like their assets professionally managed, invested, and partially distributed to the children as the children are growing up and the need arises.

Let's now have a look at a "translation," in simple English, of the will the lawyer drew up for Mr. Married. Mrs. Married's separate will would be *reciprocal*, meaning identical to Mr. Married's but with her name instead of his. (Incidentally, like all the examples in the book, this will is only illustrative and is *not* intended to be used as a form by you.)

Last Will and Testament of Mike Married

I, Mike Married, a resident of _____ , hereby make my last will and testament:
1. This will revokes all prior wills and codicils I have made.
2. I am married to Minerva Married, and I have two children from my marriage with

Minerva: John Married and Abigail Married. John's birthdate is March 20, 1984, and Abigail's birthdate is June 19, 1986. I have no other children or descendants, alive or deceased. Any children I may have or adopt in the future will be treated like the two children I now have.

3. I leave my entire estate to my wife, if she survives me.

4. If my wife does not survive me, I leave my entire estate to my half brother, PAUL SMITH, and XYZ TRUST COMPANY, to act as trustees under the following trust:

   (1) The trustees may make investments with my trust assets in any way they deem reasonable and proper.

   (2) The trustees may distribute the net income of the trust, and also principal if need be, to my two children as they are growing up, in whatever amounts are reasonable for their health, education, living expenses, support, maintenance, and travel. Distributions of a certain amount to one child will not require equal distributions to the other child. In fact, all the trust assets could be distributed to one child, and not the other, if the need exists. Before making any distributions for the above purposes, my trustee shall determine whether the child has funds reasonably accessible to him or her to use for those purposes, and if so, the trustee shall not make distributions to the child.

   (3) When each child attains the age of 24, I do not want the child to receive any more distributions from this trust until it ter-

minates, unless a distribution is necessary, in the trustee's discretion, for an emergency. It is my desire in making this statement that each child learn what it is like to make a living for himself or herself, and I don't want them to be dependent upon my trust or my assets.

(4) When the youngest child attains the age of 28, the trustee shall distribute one third of the trust in equal shares to my children who are then alive. I am making this partial distribution in the hopes that if a child squanders his or her one-third share at 28, he or she will be wiser at 33 when the rest of the trust assets are distributed.

(5) When the youngest child attains the age of 33, the trustee shall distribute the balance of my trust in equal shares to my children who are then alive.

(6) I appoint my half brother, Paul Smith, as guardian of my minor children, to serve as guardian until each child attains the age of majority. If Paul for any reason ceases to act, I appoint Minerva's sister, Mildred, as guardian.

(7) I appoint my spouse as executor, or if she for any reason cannot serve, I appoint XYZ Trust Company as executor. The executor shall serve without bond.

(8) During probate, my executor can sell any asset to raise needed funds.

Dated: _____ /s/ Mike Married

On _____ , Mike Married told us this was his will and asked us to witness his

signature. We all were together and saw him
sign his will; we believe he is over the age of
majority and of sound mind.

_____ /s/ <u>Wilma Witness</u>

_____ /s/ <u>Walter Witness</u>

_____ /s/ <u>Webley Witness</u>

Let us assume that Mike Married dies first. The only things
that Mike's will is going to control are his $15,000 of cash and
his $11,000 of miscellaneous property, because these are the
only things that he owned in his name alone. Minerva, therefore, will receive those assets under Mike's will.

After Mike's death, then, assuming that Minerva was
properly named beneficiary on Mike's life insurance and
retirement plan, and that she was the joint tenancy or tenancy by the entirety owner of all the co-owned assets that
Mike owned, Minerva will own the following assets:

ASSETS	OWNED BY HUSBAND	OWNED BY WIFE	CO-OWNERSHIP	TOTAL
Life Insurance	_____	$ 75,000	_____	$ 75,000
Cash	_____	47,000	_____	47,000
Money Market Certificates, Certificates of Deposit	_____	125,000	_____	125,000
IRA, etc.	_____	54,000	_____	54,000
Stocks & Bonds	_____	56,000	_____	56,000
Real Estate —Residence	_____	220,000	_____	220,000
—Vacation/ Rental	_____	95,000	_____	95,000

ASSETS	OWNED BY HUSBAND	OWNED BY WIFE	CO-OWNERSHIP	TOTAL
Sole Proprietorship or Partnership Interest	————	112,000	————	112,000
Miscellaneous	————	89,000	————	89,000
Life Insurance Payoff on Mike's Death	————	145,000	————	145,000
Retirement Payoff on Mike's Death	————	78,000	————	78,000
TOTAL ASSETS	————	$1,096,000	————	$1,096,000

Minerva, as you can see from the list above, now owns every asset in her name alone. When she dies later on, her will is going to control all of these assets, with the exception of her life insurance and her retirement plan monies. Her will, as we have seen above, is exactly like Mike's will, and establishes a testamentary trust for the children. She should make sure that the primary beneficiary on her life insurance and retirement plan reads: "Paul Smith and XYZ Trust Company, as Trustees of the Testamentary Trust established under my will dated _____ ." In fact, when Mike was alive, he would have named Minerva as the primary beneficiary, and Paul and XYZ as secondary or contingent beneficiaries, and Minerva would have done the same. Now that Mike's gone, Minerva can move Paul and XYZ into the primary beneficiary position.

Review

Let's stop for a minute and regroup so we can see where we are. We've learned where your assets go at your death, and how you can control where they go by joint tenancy, beneficiary designation on life insurance and retirement proceeds, and by dying with or without a will.

Now we're going to look at probate and estate taxes, which are the two biggest impediments your heirs face to receiving one hundred cents on every dollar you leave. These impediments won't take an asset and give it from one heir to another heir—you control who's getting the asset as noted above—but they can cause the heir to get less than you had when you died. And, to put probate and estate taxes in perspective, remember that there can be many other payments at your death: ambulance, hospital, doctors, funeral, burial, your debts, your income taxes for the part of the year you lived. Of all these charges against your estate, only probate and estate taxes are completely avoidable and voluntary if you take precautions ahead of time. Since probate is a kind of buzz word that people are perhaps overly concerned about, let's have a look at it first. We'll discover why a will does not avoid probate, and we'll discover how you can arrange your affairs in such a way as to completely eliminate probate.

Chapter 3

Probate

You should, by now, have filled out your checklist, distinguished between the three different types of co-owned assets you may have, and established, in a general kind of way, your objectives for your assets at your death. We've had a brief look, in the last chapter, at what a will can do to attain your objectives, and you should realize that a will is not going to control where all of your assets go. Indeed, four out of the six categories of assets are going to be controlled not by your will, but instead by your beneficiary designation, or by the form of co-ownership that you have (joint tenancy with rights of survivorship, or tenancy by the entirety). You probably also understand that there are two critters out there that are going to eat up part of your estate at your death: probate and estate taxes. Before we learn *how* to avoid the first problem, probate, let's spend a few mintues to see exactly what it is, and why most people want to avoid it.

In General

Sometimes called administration or estate administration, *probate* is a court-supervised procedure that can affect two of the six categories of your assets when you die. If you don't have an asset in these two categories, then your estate needn't go through probate. Every state has a procedure for probate, and as you would suspect, the rules and regulations for how probate is governed vary considerably from state to state. Nevertheless, there are a few generalities that can be made about the probate system, and once those generalities have been stated, you will be able to see why most people want to avoid the system entirely.

What assets does the probate system affect?

Of the six categories of assets, probate affects only two: those assets held in your name alone when you die, and your share as a tenant in common with other people. Probate will *not* be needed for life insurance proceeds, retirement plan proceeds, an asset held as a joint tenant with rights of survivorship with another person, and an asset held as tenant by the entirety with your spouse. Since assets in these latter four categories escape probate, they can be distributed immediately upon your death to the people who are entitled to them. The rest of this chapter, therefore, ignores assets in these four categories, and focuses only on solely owned assets and your share of an asset as tenant in common, which are the only probatable assets.

EXAMPLE: Jim and Sue are married. Jim has named Sue as primary beneficiary on his life insurance and retirement plan. All their stocks, bonds, bank accounts, and home are owned as joint tenants with rights of survivorship. On Jim's death, all his assets go to Sue *without probate*. Now, however, all those assets are in her name alone and, unless she takes steps to avoid it, will be probated at her death.

What is the purpose of probate?

The purpose of probate, in every state, is to take the asset out of the dead person's name and to put it in the name of a living person. (*Which* living person will get it depends on whether you had a will—which controls it and other solely owned assets—or *didn't have* a will, in which case it will go to a person on your family tree.) For example, if you should own a bank account in your name alone, it will go through probate when you die. The purpose of putting it through probate is to take the bank account out of your name (you're dead at this point, and can't use it any longer) and to put it in the name of a living person: in other words, to *clear title*.

In providing a court-supervised procedure for changing the title to an asset, probate serves to protect the institution that holds the asset.

EXAMPLE: Sam's will says, among other things, "My bank account goes to Mary upon my death." Sam owns a bank account, in his name alone. When he dies, Mary gets his will and a copy of his death certificate, walks into the bank, and asks them to turn over the bank account to her. The bank, quite properly, is going to refuse to do this for a number of reasons: How do they know that this is Sam's *last* will and testament (there could be a later one, or this one could be void because it was forged, or executed under undue influence, duress, or through fraud). How do they know this is the right "Mary"? How do they know that all Sam's debts have been paid? How do they know his estate taxes have been paid? Perhaps there was a codicil to Sam's will that Mary is not showing them. In other words, the bank needs some protection before they can distribute Sam's bank account. This protection is given them through the probate system, which, being court supervised, will assure the bank that it can release the funds to the proper person without subjecting itself to any further liability by some later claimant.

How does probate work, in general?*

Essentially, probate does three things. First, a person is appointed to gather together all of the deceased's assets that were in his name alone, or his share as a tenant in common with other people. (This person is called the *executor*.) Next, having collected all of the deceased's assets that have to go through probate, the executor assembles all debts of the deceased, pays the bills, and pays the estate taxes. (The deceased's legitimate debts and estate taxes have to be paid before any of his wealth can be distributed

* If you want a more detailed step-by-step look at the probate process, see Chapter 3 of *Who Gets It When You Go?*

to beneficiaries, who, after all, are receiving it for free.)
Finally, after the deceased's obligations and taxes are paid,
then the executor pays the balance of the assets in accordance with the deceased's will, or, if there was no will, under
the deceased's state's intestacy laws.

What's Objectionable About the Probate Process?

Heirs who have gone through the probate process generally
voice three objections to the system: It takes a long time,
it generates unwanted publicity, and it's expensive. Let's
take these three topics one by one.

The length of probate

Remembering that probate only affects assets in the deceased's name alone, or the deceased's share as a tenant in
common with other people, you might be surprised to learn
that the probate process normally takes at least a year to
complete. That means, in our example above, that Sam's
bank account is not going to be distributable to Mary until
at least a year has passed from the start of probate (not
from Sam's death, but from the *start* of the probate process
in the court system). While it's true that there could be
partial distributions of probate assets to the people that are
entitled during the course of probate, it's also true that the
executor does not *have* to make these partial distributions,
and indeed he might not make any substantial partial distributions until probate has finished and he has been authorized to distribute the balance of the estate by the probate judge.

Why does probate take so long? First, the nature of the

job itself (collecting and safeguarding assets, inventorying them, advertising for creditors to present their claims, paying creditors and taxes) takes time. Second, and perhaps more time-consuming, are the time delays the law requires of the executor (who is the individual or trust company actually doing all these probate jobs), putting notice in the paper about your probate's status, and holding the period for creditor claims open for several months (four to six months is not uncommon). Next is the overburdened court system, which appoints, supervises, and then releases the executor. Finally, if there is a probate, the executor is responsible for determining the amount of and paying estate taxes. The tax return is due nine months from death, and if probate is taking so long anyway, few executors see a need to rush to pay the taxes.

Unwanted publicity

There are two forms of publicity during the course of probate, and generally heirs don't like either one. First, because the probate process is being administered through the court system, all of the multitudinous papers that the executor files, including the deceased's will (if he had one) and an inventory of the assets going through probate, including their value, are filed with the state court system. Once they are filed, they are a part of the "public records," and anybody can get into those records and look at them. They can look at your will and see who you included and excluded. They can look at the inventory of your probate assets and see how much, or how little, you were worth. In other words, they can poke their noses into your business. Many people, and many heirs, find this quite objectionable, but the only way to avoid it is to avoid the probate system altogether. (See the next chapter.)

The second form of publicity that probate engenders is that in most states, the probate system requires the executor to publish notice in a newspaper once, twice, or even three times, notifying the general public at large as to the particular status of the probate at that point. For example, the first notice might be notifying the public that you have died, that so-and-so is attempting to be appointed as executor, and that a will has been presented to the probate court. If anyone has an objection to the executor or to the will, this notice tells him how to proceed to make his objections known to the judge. Another notice might be published notifying the public that the executor is asking for all creditor claims to be presented. Yet another notice could be required to tell everyone that the executor has finished his job, and is about ready to distribute the remaining assets in the estate. In other words, these newspaper notices keep the public notified of the progress of your probate—one more intrusion into your private, personal, and financial affairs.

The expense of probate

There can be any number of people involved in your probate proceeding: the executor; a lawyer for your executor; an appraiser for your probate property; an independent lawyer appointed by the probate court to review the accountings that your executor must keep; the court system itself. All of these people will or may (depending upon your state's own particular probate laws) have jobs to perform. They're not required to do those jobs for free, nor are they expected to do so. They're going to get paid, and their fees are going to come out of your probatable assets. The fees vary from state to state; sometimes they vary from city to city within the same state. There are various ways of calculating the fees: hourly rate, flat percentage of the asset, sliding percentage of the asset. Nevertheless, a rough ball-park figure would probably be 6 percent of your probate assets, but you should remember that your own personal probate may be more or less expensive than that.

EXAMPLE: Juliet dies, owning her home in her name alone. Since it's in her name alone, it must go through the probate system. An appraiser is appointed by the probate court, and the appraiser appraises the value of the property, as of Juliet's date of death, at $100,000. The appraiser charges a flat $150 for his appraisal. There is a $40,000 mortgage on the property. Therefore, if you think about it, Juliet's interest in the property is only $60,000; the mortgage company is owed $40,000. In Juliet's state, the executor's and attorney's fees are figured upon the entire $100,000 of appraised value. That fee, in Juliet's state, is $6,000, 10 percent of Juliet's equity.

"Okay, Now that We've Heard the Bad Stuff, What's Beneficial About the Probate System?"

During the course of probate, your executor files numerous papers with the probate court, and the judge of the probate court reviews those papers, and makes sure that your probate is proceeding according to the law. Every step of the way, the executor is filing one paper or another with the court. This makes it very difficult, perhaps even impossible, for people who are not entitled to your estate to receive any part of it. This means that greedy relatives, uncouth creditors, and other undesirables will be kept away from your estate.

Another benefit of the probate system is that it shortens the statute of limitations that your creditors have to present claims against your estate. For example, if, while you're alive, you incur some debts or injure somebody (for example, with your automobile), then those people have a right to make a claim against you (while you're alive), and after your death, against your estate. If there is no probate proceeding, then those people may have lengthy periods of time in which they can make claims against your estate and against the assets in your estate. However, with a probate proceeding, one of the first jobs of the executor in many states is to publish, in the newspaper, a "notice to creditors" that informs all of your creditors that they have a certain, shortened, period of time in which they must present their claims against you and your assets. If they do not make their claims within this shortened period of time (usually four to six months), then they aren't going to get paid, and they have no legal rights against your estate, or your assets, or your heirs. In fact, frequently probates are established in order to "smoke out" creditors, particularly if the heirs are not certain who the creditors might be, or just exactly how much they might claim.

On Balance

Even though probate can be useful to make sure that your assets get distributed exactly according to law and to keep greedy relatives away from any unauthorized share of your estate, and even though probate does shorten the period your creditors have to claim against your estate and assets, most people, on balance, find the probate procedure overlong, cumbersome, and expensive. The irony of probate is that it's only legally required for those who did not arrange their affairs in such a way as to avoid it: in other words, the ostriches among us who, knowing that this unpleasantness is going to happen to their heirs, stick their heads in the sand and don't take any action to avoid it. The next chapter is going to show you how to avoid probate, and thereby save your heirs a lot of time and a lot of money.

Chapter 4

How to Avoid Probate

If you look back at your checklist, it would be a good time at this point to see just exactly which of your assets are going to go through probate. Again, remember that if you have any assets in tenancy by the entirety or joint tenancy, these assets won't go through probate on *your* death but will go through probate upon your spouse's death or upon the joint tenant's death. Also, your life insurance and retirement proceeds, if you have named a beneficiary, will not go through probate on *your* death but will go through probate upon the surviving beneficiary's later death.

You can figure it out: If you have a bank account that's in your name, or a stock that's in your name, or a house that's in your name, or any other kind of asset that is registered solely in your name, it's going to go through probate. There are only two ways to avoid probate on these kinds of assets. First, you can reregister them by taking them out of your name alone and adding somebody else's name as a joint tenant with rights of survivorship or as a tenant by the entirety. Second, you can create a living trust.

Joint Tenancy with Rights of Survivorship

Since many, many people hold assets as joint tenants with rights of survivorship, let's spend a few minutes to see what they have gotten themselves into with resepct to this form of avoiding probate. What you will probably recognize is that, before you transfer any assets into joint tenancy or tenancy by the entirety, you had better think it through pretty carefully. While these forms of ownership will definitely avoid probate (which is good), there are numerous side effects to joint tenancy and tenancy by the entirety that may not be so good.

As a model for the following discussion, let's look back at Sally Single, whose assets appeared on page 6. You can see that most of her assets are in her name alone. That means they are going to go through probate upon her death. Sally has read this book this far and she's now considering transferring her assets into joint ownership with certain people. Let's focus on her house, which is worth approximately $150,000. What are the effects of transferring this house into joint ownership?

Pick your joint owner with care

You know that your joint owner is going to get the entire asset when you die. That's the nature of joint ownership. You also know that he or she is going to get it without probate. That's the objective you are trying to attain. Unfortunately, because of the nature of joint tenancy, your joint owner may also get a share of your asset while you're *alive*. This is because joint *tenancy* means *joint ownership*. Once you create a joint tenancy in an asset, you don't own the asset by yourself any longer; you only own a share of the asset, along with your other joint owner(s) who own their own respective share or shares. For example, if Sally adds Sam Single's name to her house as joint tenants with rights of survivorship, then Sally no longer owns all the house. She owns half the house. Her brother, Sam, owns the other half. During Sally's lifetime, the unfortunate fact is that Sam is able to do with his half of the house anything he wants. If he wants to give it away to somebody else (his wife, girl friend, daughter, a charity, etc.), he can do so, since he is the absolute owner of one half of that house.

Not only can Sam give it away, but his half of the asset can also be taken away involuntarily. If he gets divorced, the divorce judge may order him to give his half of the house to his ex-wife. Or if Sam should get into a lawsuit (let's say because of a car crash, or a slip-and-fall at his home) and is found guilty and does not have enough insurance to cover the judgment against him, his half of the house is one of the assets that his creditors might decide to take away from him. In other words, Sally, whose motives were pure as the driven snow in trying to get this house to Sam without any probate, has unwittingly given up half ownership in the house, which in turn can be taken away from Sam, or given away by him, leaving Sally with a new co-owner of the house, someone she doesn't even know. The problem only increases: In most states, a co-owner of a piece of real estate, no matter how small the proportion they own, can force the sale of the entire property, even without the remaining co-owner's permission. Therefore, Sam could force the sale of the property, or one of his creditors or transferees could. If the property is sold, then the monies received would be divided between Sally and Sam or his transferee or his creditor. This doesn't give Sally very much protection. She started out owning an entire house, which was under her sole control, and she ended up with either half a house, or half of a bucket of money.

Therefore, before you add somebody's name to an account, a stock, a bond, a piece of real estate, or anything else, just remember that you're giving up a share of the ownership. You had better trust your co-owner implicitly. You had also better be certain that your co-owner is adequately insured in case that person gets into (for example) an automobile crash, finds himself underinsured, and then has personal assets (including the half of the house that was formerly yours) taken away.

In other words, you place your assets at risk when you add another owner or owners.

You may very well be making a taxable gift when you create a joint tenancy

As we have seen in the section above, when you create a joint tenancy, you are giving something away. You are giving away a proportionate share of the value of the asset. As we will find out in the next chapter, Uncle Sam has a *gift tax*, a tax upon any kind of a gift made from one person to another. There is a $10,000 per recipient per year exemption from this, but if you give a person more than $10,000 per year, then Uncle Sam is going to tax you (the donor) on the value of the gift in excess of $10,000.

EXAMPLE: Sally decides to add Sam's name to the deed to her house as joint tenant. Her motivation is to avoid probate. Once she signs the deed adding his name, she has made a gift to Sam. To the extent that the value of one half of the house exceeds $10,000, she has made a *taxable* gift to Sam. An appraisal of the house would be made, and if half the value exceeds $10,000, Sally must file a gift tax return with the federal government.

There are only a few exceptions to this rule of "add an owner, make a gift." An added joint tenant on a bank account causes no gift until the non-depositor makes a withdrawal, or until a depositor withdraws more than he or she put in. If your stocks are held at a brokerage house, there's no gift if you add a joint tenant. And if you add another's name as joint tenant to a U.S. Savings Bond, there's no gift.

People forget that joint tenancy is not controlled by their will

This can perhaps best be seen by an example. Suppose Gertrude has a will that says, "All of my assets go to my brother, Ben." Unfortunately, Gertrude has added her sister, Sue, as joint tenant on the bank account, and also as a joint tenant on her stock and bond account at the brokerage house. She did this primarily for purposes of convenience. When she is out of town, or not feeling well, her sister can write checks, and can also play the stock market for her. However, at her death, since the bank account and the stock and bond account were held as joint tenants with rights of survivorship between Gertrude and Sue, Sue is going to get those accounts. They are not going to go to brother Ben under the provisions of Sue's will because a will does not control joint tenancy assets. This can be very frustrating to Ben, it can create friction between Ben and Sue, and the bottom line is that Gertrude's most fervent wish (that Ben get all of her estate) has been frustrated. Finally, if Sue, trying to honor Gertrude's wishes in her will, gives the bank and stock accounts to Ben—you guessed it—it could be a taxable gift.

With joint tenancy, the survivor takes all

When the first joint tenant dies, there is no probate, and the surviving joint owner takes the entire asset. It's at this point that people seem to forget what's happening: The surviving joint owner, now being the complete owner, can do anything he or she wants with the asset. This result may be quite contrary to what the first joint owner would have wished, had he or she thought it through.

EXAMPLE: A husband and wife own their house as joint tenants with rights of survivorship. The wife dies. The husband gets the entire house, without probate. The house is now in his name, and he can do anything he likes with it. He can leave it to his brother, or to his favorite charity. He doesn't *have* to leave it to anyone his wife might have wanted. He doesn't *have* to leave it to the kids. He can conveniently "forget" any understanding he and his wife may have had regarding who gets the house after they both

die. He can will it to his new wife, thereby cutting out the
children from his first marriage; he can put it in joint ownership with his new wife, thereby again cutting out the
children from his first marriage if he predeceases his new
wife; or he can do anything else he wants with that property.
Do you think that his first wife would have been happy if
she had known that this house, for which she had worked
hard all her life, might end up going to a new wife and out
of the family?

EXAMPLE: Joint tenancy is especially dangerous when we
are dealing with a second marriage for one or both of the
spouses. For example: The husband has children from his
first marriage; the wife has children from her first marriage.
The husband and wife decide to get married. The husband
brings certain assets into the marriage; the wife brings
certain assets into the marriage. The husband and wife put
all of those assets in joint ownership. If the husband dies
first, all of those assets are going to the wife. It's true that
they have avoided probate, but look at the mess they have
created now: The wife owns all of the assets and can do
anything she likes with them. She's probably not going to
leave much, if anything, of those assets to the husband's
children from his prior marriage. Why should she? They're
not related to her by any blood tie, and she may not even
like them. The husband is going to be real unhappy when
he looks up from the grave and sees this happening, but
there's nothing he, or his children, can do about it. The
husband and wife would have been much better advised to
avoid joint ownership completely. Nevertheless, because of
the common understanding among people in America that
joint ownership avoids probate, they let the tail wag the

dog, and while they did avoid probate, they got themselves into worse trouble.

Joint tenancy can cause a tax crunch

For a married couple, joint tenancy can *increase* estate taxes. Frequently, depending upon the tax objectives of a married couple, it's best to transfer assets out of joint tenancy into either the husband's name or into the wife's name. We'll learn more about this in the next chapter, so don't go rushing out to your bank or brokerage house right now and start dividing things up.

Joint tenancy is clumsy

Sally Single wants to leave her assets as follows: $10,000 to person A; $20,000 to person B; $30,000 to person C; and everything else to person D. She can clearly make a will that will achieve this objective, and the exact amounts will be paid out to the proper people, but her assets would have to go through probate. To avoid probate, she can certainly create joint tenancies: a joint tenancy in a particular account with A; another joint tenancy in another account with B; yet another one on another account with C; and finally, a joint account or accounts with respect to the rest of her assets with D. But, unfortunately, there is no assurance that the exact amounts that Sally wants to be paid to these people will in fact be the amounts in those accounts as of Sally's date of death. Depending on deposits to and withdrawals from the accounts, and investment fortunes or misfortunes, the value of those accounts can be less or more than what Sally had really wanted. Is she stuck? Is there any other way for her to get these exact amounts to these people and yet avoid probate? The answer is yes, and she can do it with a living trust, which is discussed shortly.

Having pointed out these six categories of bad things about joint tenancy, what can we say that is *good* about joint tenancy as a way to avoid probate? There are really two things: First, it's certain to work, and second, it's quite inexpensive. Ordinarily, you won't need a lawyer or any other professional assistance or expense to transfer your assets into joint names. This can be a relief, but as you probably know, you get what you pay for. Most people, after they have been educated this far on joint tenancy, want to know a little bit more about the other alternative of avoiding probate, which is a living trust.

One observation before moving on: To be frank, most of the probates are for single people. If you're married, chances are you own most of your assets in joint tenancy with your spouse. There won't be a probate when the first spouse dies, but when the survivor dies (who inherited all the assets from the deceased spouse), there will be a very large probate. Likewise, if you're a single person already, then chances are you own most of your assets in just your name. Lawyers see more probates, and larger probates, for single people than for married couples.

You might want to take a look at your own estate-planning checklist at this point, and particularly look at the people you have chosen to be joint owners. On your own, you can make up your mind whether these joint owners present any threats or difficulties to you with respect to the six problems of joint tenancy outlined above. If you think you might have a problem with your joint owner, you might be interested in reading further about a living trust.

Living Trusts Avoid Probate Without Any of the Drawbacks of Joint Ownership

You may feel "sold out" by now. You understand that a will is necessary to get your assets to the people that you want to have them, but you also understand that the only assets that a will controls are, ironically, the very ones that go through probate. So, if you want to avoid probate, you feel that you might be forced into joint tenancy, but you've read, with growing dismay, about the drawbacks of joint tenancy. Can you have it all? Can you (1) keep control of an asset during your lifetime so that no one else can tell you what to do with it, (2) avoid the other pitfalls of joint tenancy, and (3) avoid probate upon your death?

The answer is that a *living trust* can do all of these things. It will let you have total control over your assets during your life, it will avoid probate upon your death, and then it acts as a will substitute in that it distributes your assets whatever way you want, and not necessarily to one person as does a joint tenancy.

How does a living trust work? A living trust is a device for allowing yourself or another person (the trustee) to own and manage your assets for your, or for someone else's, benefit. It is established while you are living (hence, a living trust) rather than at your death (a testamentary trust). You simply give an asset to the trustee, give him or her instructions on how to manage the asset, and let the trustee go to work. What kind of asset can you give to the trustee? The answer is, anything. A stock, cash, a house, a bond, a money market certificate, a bird or birdcage—anything you can own yourself, you can transfer to the trustee.

EXAMPLE: Sam is tired of managing his rental condominium apartment. He has experienced too much hassle in getting renters, keeping them happy, paying his condo bills, and collecting his rents. He transfers ownership of the apartment to Tina Trustee, in a living trust, with whatever instructions he feels are appropriate. For example, he might give her these written directions: "Don't rent it for less than $100 a week; don't rent it for two weeks in the month of August when I plan to use it; don't sell it or rent it for more than six months without my prior permission; collect the rent, pay the mortgage and condo fees, take a reasonable trustee's fee, and send me the balance." Since all of the rental burdens have been shifted to Tina, the trustee, Sam can more avidly pursue his hobby, bird watching.

Most people who establish living trusts do two things with them. First, they retain the right to revoke or amend the trust at any time. This way, they can remove and replace the trustee, change the trust's provisions, or even revoke the entire trust if they get tired of it. The second thing is that they retain the right to all of the income that the trust assets earn. In other words, in their written instructions to the trustee, which is called the *trust agreement*, they would retain the right to receive all of the income that the trustee generated through the trustee's investments or managing the assets of the trust.

EXAMPLE: Zelda transfers all her stocks and bonds to Tim, the trustee, giving him, in the trust agreement, full authority to trade in any stock or bond Tim may choose from time to time. She also adds: "During my life, I direct the trustee to distribute all the income that the trust earns to me, at least every other month. In addition, if I ask the trustee to distribute principal [that is, the stocks or bonds themselves] to me, I expect the trustee will do this."

What happens to a living trust upon your death? Well, first of all, the assets that are in it avoid probate. But what is the trustee to *do* with those assets? The answer to this is that the trustee will continue to manage the trust in accordance with provisions you have put into the trust agreement. For example, the trustee could be required, under the terms of the trust agreement, to continue to hold and manage the assets, or he could be required to disburse the assets. In the following example, both these things are done.

EXAMPLE: Zelda adds these provisions to her trust agreement: "Upon my death, I want the trustee to disburse out of the trust $10,000 to person A, $20,000 to person B, and to keep the balance of the trust's assets in a continuing trust. This continuing trust is to be operated and managed by my trustee for the benefit of my two children, Paul and Jill. The trustee is to disburse to Paul and Jill whatever amounts of income or principal are in the trust as the trustee determines, in its discretion, to be appropriate for their health and further education. When both of them have reached the age of 28, I want the trustee to distribute the assets that are then remaining, half to each one of them, or if one has died, all to the survivor."

In other words, after your death, the living trust acts just like your will in that it disburses your assets in accordance with written directions. The major difference, though, between a trust and a will is that the trust avoids probate while the will doesn't.

An extra bonus: your incompetency

Look back for a second at Sally Single's checklist on page 6. Note all of those assets that she owns in her name alone. Since they are solely in her name, only she has the right to manage them and to deal with them. But what happens if she becomes incapacitated, either mentally or physically? Someone is going to have to step in and manage them for her. There are only three ways that this can be done: (1) A guardian could be appointed through the probate court system; (2) Sally could have created a durable power of attorney that named somebody to manage these assets upon the incompetency; and (3) if the assets were in a living trust, the trustee would manage them for her during Sally's incapacity.

The first way, establishing guardianship through a probate court hearing, is the worst of the three ways, since it is expensive (a lawyer needs to be hired, and a separate *guardian ad litem* would probably have to be appointed by the court to report back to the judge regarding whether or not Sally really is incapacitated). In addition, a guardianship will require an annual accounting by the guardian, which will cost more money to prepare and then present (again with a lawyer) to the judge.

The second alternative, a durable power of attorney, is available in many states. The word *durable* simply means that the power of attorney will still be good even if Sally should become incapacitated. Under the former law in many states, a power of attorney would become invalid when Sally became incapacitated, which was, oddly enough, exactly the time that it was most needed. But many states have now passed laws that allow the power of attorney to work even after Sally's incapacity. A sample power of attorney would be something along the following lines, all provisions of which are optional:

> I, SALLY SINGLE, hereby appoint Arthur Smith and give him the following authority:
> 1. To buy, sell, trade, exchange, mortgage, lease, or transfer any of my assets, whether real estate, stocks, bonds, or personal property. [If Sally wanted to restrict Arthur more than this, she could give him only limited powers: "only to sell my car, Honda # ABC1234."]
> 2. To consent to any medical treatments that may be necessary for me.
> 3. During my incapacity, to make gifts to people in my family.
> 4. To enter into, withdraw from, and deposit into any bank accounts, safe-deposit boxes, or savings and loan accounts that I may have.
> 5. This power of attorney shall become effective only upon my incapacity. My incapacity shall be proven by a written statement from my physician stating that I am no longer competent to manage my business affairs. [Or Sally could have inserted: "This power of attorney shall become effective immediately, and my incapacity, either mental or physical, shall not affect its validity."]

> Dated: _____ at _____ .

> _____
> SALLY SINGLE

This problem with a power of attorney is that it is only valid as long as Sally is alive. The instant she dies, Arthur

Smith no longer has any authority whatsoever to transact business on her behalf. He cannot get into her bank accounts, he cannot sell her house, he cannot trade her stock, he cannot enter into her safe-deposit box, etc. From the moment of her death forward, only her executor can do those things, and as we have seen, it requires a probate proceeding to create an executor. Therefore, the power of attorney will not help clean up her business matters after she dies, it will not avoid probate, and it will not serve to direct where her assets will go after she dies; only a will or living trust can do that.

The third alternative to dealing with one's assets upon incapacity, a living trust, is probably cheaper than a guardianship (alternative #1) and more expensive than a power of attorney (alternative #2), but unlike either of those two alternatives, neither of which would avoid a probate of your assets upon your death, a living trust will avoid probate. The way the living trust works is that Sally simply puts a provision in her living trust that says, "If I should become incapacitated, either mentally or physically, then I want my trustee, John Jones, to manage the assets of this trust in such a way as will best provide for my needs." Sally gets the extra benefit of a living trust in that it will avoid probate when she dies.

Another bonus: better protection for your objectives

Everyone has heard of will contests. They are brought by a disappointed heir who tries to show either that (1) your will was not executed in strict compliance with your state's laws (for example, your state requires three witnesses and you had only two) or (2) when you signed your will, you did not have the required mental ability because of senility, drugs, alcohol, fraud, undue influence, or duress. If the contesting heir is successful on either of those grounds, your will is invalidated by the probate court, and you either die intestate or, if you had an earlier will, it might come into play.

Certain situations seem to breed will contests. If a spouse dies and leaves a large inheritance to a second or later spouse, children from an earlier marriage could get angry. If unequal shares are left to the children, one or more might object. If an asset is left out of the family (to a friend, paramour, charity, etc.), grumblings can begin. If unusual provisions are attached to a bequest (for example, "Jimmy gets $50,000 when he graduates from veterinary school"— but Jimmy has always been a violinist), someone might be angry. All these possibilities place your will in a high-risk situation. The contestant may not prove his case and win, but your executor will have to hire an attorney and defend your will, an extra cost that will come out of your estate. How can all this be avoided, and the expense saved? A living trust, while really a substitute for a will, is far less likely to be successfully attacked than is a will. Only rarely have embittered heirs been able to invalidate living trusts, so if your objectives put your estate in jeopardy, you should definitely consider a living trust.

Choosing a trustee for your living trust

The trustee of your trust is a very important person, since the trustee actually *owns* the assets you have transferred to the trust. You had better trust your trustee! Furthermore, since your trustee will be in charge of managing your assets (selling, trading, buying, mortgaging, renting, etc., if you give your trustee those powers), you obviously need someone not only whose honesty you trust, but whose financial expertise you respect. Note that it's not necessary to give the trustee broad powers over the trust assets. You could limit the trustee in any way you want, for example: "The trustee shall make no change in trust assets without my prior written permission," or "The trustee may sell my stocks and bonds, but may reinvest only in stock in companies whose net worth exceeds $5 million." However, if you trust your trustee, and you should, you will probably want to give the trustee discretion to make investments. Finally, as in Zelda's trust, just above, which continues on for her children after her death, the trustee may have discretion to distribute principal and income to your beneficiaries after you're dead. This power demands a lot of plain old common sense as well as constant monitoring of the beneficiaries' needs.

Who should you choose as your trustee? Let's start with who you *can* choose. You are allowed to pick any adult person or any bank or trust institution qualified under state law. You can pick one or more people; you can pick a person or persons and a bank or trust company in combination. If you do pick more than one trustee, unless you put a provision to the contrary right in your trust agreement, all trustees are going to have to agree on every piece of business with respect to your trust. They are going to have to agree on what assets to sell, what assets to buy, what distributions to make to which beneficiaries, and so on. Therefore, if you do name more than one person, you might want to give one of them, by a written instruction in the trust agreement, the "controlling vote" in case the trustees can't agree on a particular matter.

Many people do select two or more co-trustees, and often

include a corporate trustee as one of the trustees for the purpose of getting the experience and expertise that a corporate trustee often can bring. However, if you want to name a person as your trustee, then be sure to provide for a successor trustee who would take over if your named trustee should for any reason (sickness, death, moving away, fatigue, etc.) cease to act.

Finally, in many states you can name yourself as your sole trustee. This enables you to (1) have the advantages of a living trust, (2) retain control over all your assets rather than allowing some other person or institution to have that control, and (3) save the fees you'd have to pay someone else, or an institution, to act as trustee for you. In fact, self-trustee trusts are enormously popular.* Frankly, there is no reason to name some other person or institution as trustee if you're able to manage your own business affairs right now. You would simply name a successor trustee, right in the trust agreement, to take over as trustee upon your incompetency or death and run the trust in accordance with the written directions that are included in the trust.

Here's an example of a self-trustee living trust for a single person. (Living trusts, of course, can be established for married couples. However, federal estate tax considerations come into play, so the use of living trusts for husband and wife is discussed on pages 102 through 105.)

---

* If your state doesn't allow self-trustee trusts, you could consider becoming a co-trustee with your spouse, friend, child, relative, etc.

Sally Single Revocable Living Trust Agreement

I, SALLY SINGLE, hereby create the "Sally Single Revocable Living Trust." I name Sally Single as trustee.

While I am alive and competent, I reserve the right to do with the trust assets whatever I wish. I can remove the income that the trust assets earn, and I can remove the principal if I wish.

While I am alive and competent, I reserve the right to amend any of the trust's provisions or even revoke the trust entirely.

While I am alive but incapacitated (either physically or mentally), then I want my successor trustee, named below, to manage my trust assets, hereby giving him full authority to sell, trade, or otherwise dispose of any of my assets, and I want him to use the income from the trust assets, and the trust assets themselves, if necessary, to provide for my health, welfare, maintenance, support, care, and comfort.

When I die, I want my successor trustee to take over the trust and to distribute the trust assets as follows: 15% of the trust assets shall be distributed to The American Red Cross, national office; 25% of the trust assets shall be distributed to my sister, Ethel Williams, or if she is then deceased, to her descendants, per stirpes; and the balance of the trust shall be retained, in a continuing trust, the provisions of which are as follows:

I want the trustee to divide the balance of my trust estate, after I have died, in three equal separate subtrusts, one for each of my three

children, Abby, Ben, and Carol. I am creating
separate but equal subtrusts, rather than keeping all the assets in a single pot, because of the
greatly differing ages and needs of my three
children, and I don't want distributions to one
child to reduce another child's inheritance, nor
do I want the oldest child to have to wait until
the youngest child grows up before he can receive his share of my estate outright. As each is
growing up, I want the trustee to use income
and principal of each subtrust for the respective
child's education, health, and ordinary and
usual living expenses. However, as each child
attains the age of 24, I don't want any further
distributions made to that child until the subtrust terminates later on. The reason I am putting this provision in is to try to force each
child, after he or she attains the age of 24, to
get out and make his or her own living, and not
be totally dependent upon my trustee and my
estate for a livelihood. Nevertheless, after a
child does attain the age of 24, if the trustee determines that such child has an emergency,
then the trustee may make a distribution from
the child's subtrust of income or principal to the
child to alleviate such emergency.

In determining whether a distribution to a
child is to be made at any time at all, the
trustee shall take into consideration other funds
that are readily available to that child. Distributions to my three children need not be kept
equal. No distributions shall be made to a child
from another child's subtrust, no matter what
the need.*

As each child attains the age of 30 years,

* Compare this trust's provisions to the one on p. 38, paragraph 4(2).

then the subtrust shall terminate and the trustee shall distribute whatever is remaining in the subtrust to the child. If a child dies before reaching 30, his or her subtrust shall go to his or her issue, per stirpes, or if there are no such issue alive, then to the subtrusts for my remaining two children, or if a subtrust has ended, to the child himself or herself.

I name John Smith as my successor trustee, to take over upon the date I, for any reason, cease to act as trustee. If John for any reason ceases to act, then I name ABC Trust Company to take over as successor trustee. No trustee shall be required to post bond.

The powers of my trustees are as follows: They can buy, sell, trade, mortgage, lease, rent, or do anything else with my real estate and personal property they wish. Just as a matter of suggestion, and not as a requirement, I would note that I have retained an excellent stockbroker whose name is Susan Sanders, and I would suggest that my trustees use her services in determining whether any of my stocks are to be sold or retained.

Dated: _____   _____
                             SALLY SINGLE,
                             Settlor

                             _____
                             SALLY SINGLE,
                             Trustee

Let's have a look at two items in this trust. First, you'll notice that Sally retained the right to revoke the trust or to amend it. Most living trusts that are created these days are indeed revocable and amendable. Like most people, Sally doesn't want to get locked into something she can't change in the future. For example, her three children may, down the road, have vastly differing needs than they do now, so Sally would like to be able to change her trust agreement to reflect those new circumstances. In fact, there are very few reasons to create irrevocable, unamendable trusts, and we'll learn about most of them in the next chapter.

Second, you will note that Sally's trust continues on after her death, and in effect acts just like Sally's will. Therefore, you really need a lawyer at this point to help you decide what provisions to put in, how to handle certain bequests, how to treat your children, etc. Just as you need a lawyer to help guide you through the maze of possibilities for your will, you also need a lawyer to help you with your living trust. While it's true that you *can* make a living trust without a lawyer's help, just as you *can* make a will without a lawyer's help, what's really important about a trust and a will are the wisdom and thoughtfulness that went into the dispositive provisions of the document, in other words, who gets what, and when they get it. And when we get to the next chapter, on taxes, you'll quickly see the necessity of a lawyer to dot every *i* to keep the IRS at bay. Again, a lawyer who is trained in this area will have seen many more wills and trusts than you are likely ever to see, and will have a great deal more experience in this area than you are ever likely to have. In this area, as in most areas of life, an ounce of experience is worth a bucket of brains.

• • •

Funding the Trust

Having signed her trust, Sally comes to a very critical point: She now has to change the title on her various assets over into the name of her trust. This act, called *funding*, is one that most people stub their toes on, and yet following through on this is probably the easiest part of creating a trust. Sally must actually change the registered title on her various solely owned assets by taking the title out of her name and putting it into the name of "Sally Single Revocable Living Trust." She should go to the bank, her stockbroker, her bond broker, and her savings and loan, give each of those persons a copy of her trust, and ask them to transfer her account over into the name of "Sally Single Revocable Living Trust." With respect to any real estate she might own, she can ask her lawyer, who drew up her trust for her, or her real estate agent or escrow company, to create a deed that will transfer her real estate into her living trust. Incidentally, if she has a mortgage on her property, she should be very careful to get the mortgage company's approval before she transfers her property into the trust, or she may unwittingly cause a default on her mortgage, meaning that the mortgage company can call the balance of her mortgage due even though she has kept her mortgage payments current. She should also be careful if she has any title insurance on her real estate, so that the title insurance company will continue to give her title insurance on the property after it is put into her living trust. In other words, changing title to real estate into her trust is somewhat tricky, and Sally ought to ask her lawyer to help her out in this area.

Finally, note that Sally may feel a little uncomfortable in giving each of these institutions a copy of her trust, because it contains all of her dispositive wishes on her death. Most institutions, she will be happy to learn, do not require a copy of the full trust, but only a copy of those provisions that show (1) who the present trustee and successor trustee are, and (2) what powers and authorities the trustees have with respect to the trust assets.

As she changes title to asset after asset, Sally should keep a log, or inventory, of the various items that are registered in her trust's name. Then, when the successor trustee takes over, it will know immediately what's in the trust and what it is responsible for.

Any assets that do not have the title registered in the trust's name will have to go through probate when Sally dies. Merely having a living trust is not enough if Sally does not take the extra step of changing title on her assets over into the name of her living trust. Therefore, on any assets purchased in the future, or any new accounts opened, Sally should be sure to take title in the name of "Sally Smith Revocable Living Trust." Unfortunately, many people forget to register all their assets, or newly acquired assets, in the name of their trust. Those assets will need a will to guide where they go at death, and since the objectives of Sally's estate plan have been put into her living trust, it would be appropriate for those assets to be added to the trust so they can be dealt with there as part of Sally's overall plan. Therefore, Sally's will should be a "pourover" will, one that takes the assets not already in the trust and, after probating them, "pours them over" into her trust, adding them to the trust assets so the trustee can deal with the whole kit and kaboodle in a centralized, unified way. Most states allow these "pourover" wills; check with your local attorney.

What about Sally's life insurance policies and her pension benefits? Here is another area where the living trust is better than a simple will. You may remember that a will cannot control who gets these two assets, or at what age they get them, unless they're payable to her estate, and then they have to go through probate. However, if Sally changes the beneficiary on her life insurance policy and retirement policy over to the "Sally Single Revocable Living Trust," then upon her death, the life insurance money and the retirement proceeds will be paid to her trust without probate, where they can be dealt with by her trustee in accordance with Sally's written directions right in the trust document. You can see how the living trust forms a kind of funnel for most of Sally's assets, thereby serving to coordinate and centralize her own thinking and estate planning.

Finally, what is Sally to do with respect to any assets held as joint tenant with another person? She knows that these assets won't go through probate. She also knows that when she dies, these assets will go immediately to her surviving joint owner. Since the assets will avoid probate, and will go immediately to the surviving joint owner, Sally may not want to think about having these assets, or her share of them, put into her living trust. However, she should remember that if she dies and the assets go to the surviving joint owner, then they belong to the surviving joint owner, and the surviving joint owner can do with the assets whatever he or she wishes.

EXAMPLE: Sally owns a condominium apartment at a resort with her neighbor, Helen. They took title to this condominium as joint tenants with rights of survivorship. Upon

Sally's death, the entire condominium apartment will go to Helen, without probate. At that point, Helen would be free to do with the condominium as she wishes, including leaving it to any person she wishes. In other words, after Sally dies, the apartment is out of her control. If she doesn't like this and is worried about it, then she can take her share of the apartment, put it in her living trust, and tell the trustee how she wants it dealt with upon her death. For example, she could tell the trustee to allow Helen to live in the condominium for the rest of Helen's life, but when Helen dies, to give her share to Sam Spade, her financial advisor.

You can see how easy it is to coordinate all six categories of assets with a living trust. We saw earlier how difficult it was for a will to coordinate all six categories; indeed, a will can only directly control two of the six categories, and those categories that it does control have to go through probate. A living trust can coordinate six out of the six categories and avoid probate in the bargain.

The federal income tax and your state income tax

Since your living trust assets will be earning income, interest, dividends, rentals, etc., you may be wondering whether you have to report these to the Internal Revenue Service and to your own state. Of course you do. However, if you are the trustee or co-trustee of your living trust, and if it is revocable, then you do not have to file a separate federal income tax return for your trust. You simply report all the trust's income on your own Form 1040 for the federal government. If somebody else is a trustee of your trust, then he or she must file a separate trust income tax return, called Form 1041. Whether your trust has to file a separate form (1041) or not, all income of your trust is actually taxable to you. Therefore, you are not gaining any income tax advantage by establishing a revocable living trust.

Each state has its own rules with respect to how you report the income from a revocable living trust. Many follow the federal rules. However, you should check with your state's department of taxation to be sure that you don't need an extra form, and to be sure that all the income that your trust earns is going to be taxable to you, rather than at some extra or special rate.

Overview of the Living Trust

The revocable living trust allows you to do things with your assets no other legal device allows: It gives you 100 percent control while you're alive and competent, provides for an immediate and inexpensive transition of asset management if you become incompetent, avoids probate on your death, and then distributes your assets in whatever way you want. But it's not free. It will cost attorney's fees to draft it, trustee's fees to manage it (unless you are your own trustee or a friend or family member is), and possibly tranfer fees to reregister assets into its name. It will take time to get it all done. You should determine, on your own, how these fees and time spent compare to the delay, publicity, and cost of probate. Most people opt for the living trust, but your estate may not require one. An attorney can advise you more fully.

Now let's shift the focus to the last bugaboo, the federal estate tax. To get oriented, you should know that probate and the estate tax are entirely separate and have nothing to do with each other. For example, you can avoid probate but get clobbered with the estate tax, or vice versa. But the nice thing is that, like probate, the estate tax can be avoided; it may require more than a living trust to do it, but it can be done!

Chapter 5

The Federal Estate Tax

In Perspective

The federal estate tax is a tax upon your *estate*, meaning the wealth that you leave when you die. You add up the dollar value of things you leave behind you, subtract your debts, and the balance is subject to tax. Whether you have a will is immaterial; whether you go through probate is immaterial. The question the tax man starts with is: What was the value of the things the dead guy left behind?

The tax is all-inclusive. It taxes all six categories of your assets. It taxes all of your solely owned assets that you leave; it taxes your share of any asset that you own as a tenant in common with another person; it taxes your life insurance at its face value (i.e., the amount that is paid to your beneficiary); it taxes your retirement plan proceeds; it taxes your assets that are held as joint tenants with rights of survivorship, or as tenancy by the entirety. But before you panic, be aware that there are certain exemptions and deductions, which we will learn about shortly. And even if your estate is large enough to exceed the exemptions and the deductions, there are other perfectly legal, and frequently used, methods to avoid the estate tax, which we will also learn about.

Now might be a good time for you to look at your own checklist to see what you would leave behind if you were to die tomorrow. Just add up the value of all your assets; for estate tax purposes, you are allowed to subtract any mortgages or debts, so what we are really looking for here is the net value of your estate that you are going to leave if you should die. If you are married, it would be helpful for you to add up not only what you personally are able to leave if you were to die tomorrow, but also assume that both you and your spouse were to die together, and determine the net value of the assets you and your spouse would be able to leave.

The federal estate tax law treats people differently, depending on whether they're single or married. So let's start out with the easier of the two, the single decedent. Incidentally, married persons should read this also, since many of you are going to be single when you die.

· · ·

If You Are Single

If you are single, then the federal estate tax exemption for your estate is $600,000.* In other words, you are allowed to leave behind you $600,000 worth of assets without any federal estate tax being imposed upon your heirs. Before you get too elated at this large exemption, please understand that it is an exemption against the total net value of every asset that you leave. Therefore, be sure to add up today's fair market value of your solely owned assets, your life insurance proceeds, your retirement benefits, your share as a tenant in common, and the entire value of an asset that is held as joint tenant with another person. (Since you're not married, there can't be any tenancy by the entirety asset.)

If you look back at Sally Single's checklist on page 6, you will see that the total *net* value of her estate is $300,000. Notice that she added in her life insurance proceeds and her retirement plan proceeds. Contrary to popular belief, those two categories *are* subject to estate tax. Because her total net estate is less than $600,000, the heirs of her estate will not have to pay any federal estate tax. Are there any other taxes? Yes. Her heirs may have to pay a *state* inheritance tax, depending upon the rules of the state in which Sally had her residence. But since these rules vary from state to state, and since the state inheritance tax is usually substantially less than the federal estate tax, we won't go into them here. Do the heirs pay an income tax on the assets they receive? In other words, if an heir receives, say, $100,000

---

* There is also an unlimited deduction for assets left to a charity by either single or married persons. See pages 136 through 138.

from Sally's estate, does the heir have to declare that $100,000 on his or her own tax return? The answer is no, but once the heir invests the assets, he or she has to pay an income tax on the earnings.

Let's have a closer look at how a jointly owned asset is taxed in an estate. First, if the asset is owned by Sally and another person as tenants in common, then only Sally's share of the asset is appraised at her death, and that fractional share's value is reported to the tax man.

EXAMPLE: Sally and Jim own a condominium as tenants in common. Sally owns 60 percent, and Jim owns 40 percent. On Sally's death, the condominium is appraised, and 60 percent of its value is reported to the Internal Revenue Service on Sally's estate tax return.

What happens when Sally owns an asset as joint tenant with rights of survivorship with another person? Here, the rule is more detrimental. The entire asset is appraised, and Sally's estate tax return must include *all* of the value of the asset unless Sally's executor can *prove* to the Internal Revenue Service that Sally contributed only a portion of the purchase price and improvements on the property.

EXAMPLE: Sally and Jim own a condominium apartment as joint tenants with rights of survivorship. The deed says so. On Sally's death, the condominium is appraised for $50,000. Sally's executor must report the entire value of the condominium to Uncle Sam, and have it count toward Sally's $600,000 exemption, unless the executor can *prove*, by canceled checks or other evidence, that Sally in fact only owned and paid for 60 percent of the condominium. If the executor can prove that, then only 60 percent (or $30,000) would be includable on Sally's tax return.

Now for some really good news. Unless Sally's total net estate exceeds the exemption amount ($600,000), Sally's executor does not even need to file an estate tax return.

Finally, remember that *who* gets Sally's assets depends upon the things that we've already learned, and has nothing to do with the estate tax. Also remember that whether Sally goes through probate doesn't have anything to do with the taxes that her heirs may have to pay. We hope that she had the sense to create a living trust to avoid probate, because if she didn't, then that's just one more hardship that her heirs are going to have to go through when she dies. And if her estate exceeds $600,000, not only are they going to have a probate to go through, but they're going to be facing a substantial estate tax.

If you are a single person and your net estate is under $600,000, then there's no need for you to read any further unless you just happen to be curious. On the other hand, if you're a single person with a net estate of more than $600,000, then don't despair. There are numerous ways that the tax man can be beaten, and we'll look at them shortly.

Once your estate exceeds the $600,000 level, the taxes begin at 40 percent on the excess. They can go as high as 50 percent on the excess.

EXAMPLE: Let's assume that Sally Single, instead of having a net estate of $300,000, has a net estate of $800,000. Upon her death, unless she does some tax planning as we will discuss shortly, her heirs will receive a single $600,000 exemption, and $200,000 of her estate will be subject to the tax. The tax is roughly 40 percent, so approximately $80,000 of estate taxes will have to be paid to the federal government, meaning her heirs will pocket $720,000 instead of $800,000. Exactly *which* of Sally's heirs will pay that $80,000 depends upon Sally's will; in her will she can allocate the tax burden among the people she wants to share it. If she does not do so, then her state of residence will have rules regarding who pays what amount of tax. For example, a state could require that each heir pay a pro rata amount of the tax, depending on the value of the asset each receives to the total value of the net estate. If Sally doesn't want these state rules to apply to the allocation of her tax burden, then she can designate, right in her will, who is supposed to pay her tax.

Notice that the $600,000 exemption is not for each heir; instead, it's per dead person. In other words, no matter how many different people Sally leaves her estate to, her estate is only going to have a single $600,000 exemption.

Estate Taxes for Married Couples

Married couples have two separate exemptions from the estate tax.* These can be tricky, so watch them carefully. The first exemption is that, for the spouse who dies first, whatever assets are left to the surviving spouse are completely free of any estate tax.

EXAMPLE: The husband has $6 million worth of assets, all of which are in his name. When he dies, his will says

---

* They also, like a single person, have an unlimited charitable exemption. See pages 136 through 138.

that all of those assets go to his wife. There will not be any federal estate tax at all, since whatever assets go to the surviving spouse are estate tax free. There would, however, be a horrendously large probate since all of the assets were in the husband's name. He should have established a living trust to avoid probate. (This example shows you, then, that probate and estate taxes *are* different!)

The other exemption that married couples get is that each married person also gets a $600,000 exemption for any assets left to persons *other than* the spouse.

EXAMPLE: The husband has $6 million in cash, and an additional $600,000 in stocks. He leaves the $6 million in cash to his wife (no estate tax there), and leaves the $600,000 in stocks to the children. The children receive their stocks free of federal estate tax, inasmuch as each person who dies can leave a total of $600,000 to one or more non-spouse recipients. Notice, again, that the $600,000 exemption is for the person who dies, not for each recipient who receives assets from the deceased.

Now, take a breath, shift gears, and let's see how married couples use these two exemptions. The catch is that while you can leave your spouse limitless amounts of wealth free of federal estate taxes, your spouse *is* going to die later on. And when your spouse does die later on, he or she will be limited only to a single $600,000 exemption. This is assuming, of course, that your spouse does not remarry and leave all of the assets to the new spouse. If that were to happen, then it's true that there would be no estate tax when your spouse died later on, but it would also be true that the assets would have gone out of your family.

EXAMPLE: A husband and wife own $1 million worth of assets. Some are in the husband's name, some are in the wife's name, and some are held in joint tenancy or tenancy by the entirety. When the husband dies, his will is arranged in such a way that all of his assets go to his wife. As you can see, there would be no federal estate tax at that point, because everything that the dead husband had went to his wife, and he therefore received a complete federal estate tax deduction.

Now, however, the wife owns $1 million worth of assets. She knows that when she dies, she wants all of her assets to go to her three children, equally. As we have discussed above, she is going to get only a single $600,000 exemption. Her estate is $400,000 in excess of the exemption, so that $400,000 will be fully subject to the federal estate tax. The federal estate tax is approximately 40 percent. (It increases up to a maximum of 50 percent if your estate exceeds $2.5 million but, for simplicity's sake, for the rest of the book let's pretend it's a flat 40 percent.) In other words, when the wife dies, her $1 million will go to the three children, but there will be a $160,000 federal estate tax (i.e., $1,000,000 minus $600,000 = $400,000 × .40 = $160,000 in tax).

You can see, then, that the *unlimited marital deduction* (which is the technical term for the free passing of wealth between spouses) is a mixed blessing. While it's wonderful for the surviving spouse to receive everything free of estate tax when the first spouse dies, it's entirely possible that the surviving spouse will end up with more than $600,000 of assets, meaning that, unless the surviving spouse does something quickly, there will be a federal estate tax upon her/his later death.

An approach to solving marital estate tax difficulties

Since there need not be any estate tax on the death of the first spouse, the real key is to determine whether there will be any tax on the death of the surviving spouse. Clearly, this depends upon the value of the assets the surviving spouse has to give away to the children (or to anyone else). If you would look back at your own checklist, now would be a good time to ascertain how much the surviving spouse would have to leave to your ultimate beneficiaries. Since we don't know which of the two spouses is going to die first and which is going to die second, let's simply take this approach: Add up all of the assets that the husband has, that the wife has, and that are owned jointly, then subtract all mortgages and debts. This is your net total wealth that, after you have both died, is going to be left to the children (or to the brothers, sisters, aunts, uncles, etc.). This amount is the total amount that will be available to give out after you have both died. Call it your "net family wealth."

Let's now look at three different scenarios, based upon three different net family wealths: (a) for less than $600,000; (b) for between $600,000 and $1,200,000; and (c) for net family wealth in excess of $1,200,000.

For a married couple with a net family wealth of less than $600,000

Suppose that a husband and wife look at their checklist, add up all of their assets, subtract all of their present liabilities, and determine that if they both died tomorrow, the total amount of insurance, retirement plans, jointly owned assets, and solely owned assets would be less than $600,000—let's say, for this example, $500,000. Their planning could be as follows. First, with respect to the federal estate taxes, they know that they can leave each other limitless amounts of wealth. Unfortunately, they don't have limitless amounts of wealth! "All" they have is $500,000. Nevertheless, they can certainly set up their will and trust and estate planning in such a way that, when the first of them dies, all of the assets go immediately to the survivor. There would be no tax at that point. They also know that the survivor would then have $500,000 of assets in her/his name. They know that this is below the $600,000 exemption that the survivor will have, so there will not be any federal estate tax when the survivor dies. In other words, this married couple doesn't have to take any special precautions to avoid the tax; they are below the applicable exemptions, and therefore they don't need to worry about federal estate taxes at all. (Of course, it is possible that during the surviving spouse's remaining lifetime, she/he will increase the value of those assets from the present $500,000 to over $600,000 through prudent management and wise investments, but if that happens, then while it is true that there could be a tax when the surviving spouse dies, there are also ways to avoid that tax, which we will discuss a little later on.)

Now that the married couple understands that there aren't going to be any estate tax consequences of dying, are they home free? Not yet—they still have to avoid probate. There are two ways they can do this. First, while they are both living, they could put all their assets in joint tenancy or tenancy by the entirety. They have read pages 54 through 61, and fully understand all the warnings made there about joint tenancy, but they are not concerned. When the first spouse dies, because all assets are then in joint tenancy or tenancy by the entirety, there would be no probate and the surviving spouse would automatically receive all the assets. (We also know, from the paragraph above, that there are no federal estate taxes.) The surviving spouse would then own all $500,000 of assets in her/his name alone. That spouse should then race into a lawyer's office to establish a living trust; this will avoid probate on the surviving spouse's death. In the unlikely event that they die together (actuaries say that there is less than a one percent chance of a married couple dying together or even within one year of each other), or if the surviving spouse fails to establish a living trust, then when the surviving spouse dies, there will be a probate of those assets before they can be passed on to the heirs.

Suppose, instead, that the couple has read pages 54 through 61 on joint tenancy, and they've decided they don't want joint tenancy because, sad to say, each is suspicious that the survivor will "blow" the entire pot of wealth or, in the survivor's will or trust, leave it out of the family. In more concrete terms, the wife doesn't want the husband to get her $250,000 when she dies because she's worried he'll remarry and leave it all to his new wife, cutting out her two children from a prior marriage; the husband doesn't want to leave his $250,000 to the wife because, if he dies first, he's worried she'll leave nothing to their child (his favorite), Angelique. In other words, we have here a couple that wants to ensure that, as each dies, certain assets go to certain people and not elsewhere. Joint tenancy or tenancy by the entirety is *not* for them. Instead, each should establish a separate living trust (to avoid probate), put his/her wealth into it, and at death provide that the trust's wealth would go immediately to whatever children he/she wanted. There would be no estate tax on the death of either spouse, since each left less than $600,000. The harsh fact about this approach, however, is that the surviving spouse would be unable to use or derive benefits from the deceased spouse's $250,000. If the husband or wife wanted to (1) provide for the surviving spouse and (2) ensure something is left over for the favored children, they can do it by means of a bypass trust, a QTIP trust, or a variation on either, both of which are discussed shortly.

For married couples with net family wealth of between $600,000 and $1.2 million

In this case, the simple approach of the couple described above isn't going to work. The reason is as follows: *If* the first spouse who dies leaves everything to the surviving spouse, then the surviving spouse is going to have an estate of over $600,000. Since the only exemption the surviving spouse will receive upon her/his later death will be $600,000, that will automatically mean that there will be an overage, and therefore an inheritance tax payable.

EXAMPLE: A husband and wife look at their checklist and determine that their net family wealth is $1.1 million. If the husband were to die first, and had set up his will and planning in a way that all of his wealth went to his wife, then while there would be no tax upon his death, the unfortunate fact is that the wife would be left with $1.1 million worth of assets. If she turns around and dies owning that large an estate, there is only a single $600,000 exemption, which means that $500,000 will be taxable at the 40 percent rate, and that would equal a $200,000 tax for her heirs to pay.

That means that instead of inheriting $1.1 million, the heirs would only inherit $900,000, since the federal estate tax is paid "off the top," meaning paid out of the estate before the balance of the assets are distributed to the heirs.

It's quite true that the wife could diminish her estate from $1.1 million down to $600,000 during her remaining lifetime. She can gift it away in $10,000 increments (more on this later). She can also consume $500,000 worth of assets by living and eating extravagantly. (She cannot "consume" that amount of wealth by simply changing assets. For example, taking $500,000 in cash and purchasing a $500,000 house does nothing more than change cash to bricks and mortar. When she dies, *everything* she owns will be appraised, added up, and a tax paid if over $600,000.)

Most married couples assume that the surviving spouse will not be able to gift or consume any large amounts above $600,000 during her or his remaining lifetime. (The surviving spouse might die very shortly thereafter, or the long habits of frugality built up over a lifetime might make it simply impossible for the surviving spouse to live "that well.") Consequently, for families in this bracket, between $600,000 and $1.2 million, there is going to be a tax if the surviving spouse is left with too large an estate.

One way to avoid the tax is as follows: When the first spouse dies, don't give the surviving spouse very much or anything at all! If, for example, thinking of the couple described above, the husband has $600,000 of assets, and the wife has $500,000 of assets, the tax could be avoided by the following ploy. The husband provides in his will that when he dies, his $600,000 of assets immediately go to the children. There would be no tax here because of the husband's $600,000 exemption. The wife can then live on her remaining

$500,000 and, when she dies later on, provide in her will that her $500,000 goes to her children also. There would be no tax at this point, either, because of the wife's $600,000 exemption.

The fatal flaw in this kind of planning, as you probably guessed, is that the surviving spouse is very rarely happy with less than the whole enchilada. In other words, the wife doesn't want the husband's $600,000 to go to the children at his death; she wants it to come to her. But we've seen just above that if it does come to her, then her estate is going to be inflated above $600,000, and the children will have to pay a tax when she dies. Or will they? Let's look at the following device that is frequently used to avoid taxes for people in this second bracket.

The key here is that we don't want the surviving spouse to inherit from the deceased spouse any amount of assets that would boost her/his estate over the $600,000 level. But if we don't leave those assets directly to the spouse, how can we be sure that the surviving spouse has the *use* of those assets during her/his remaining lifetime? What we use here is a trust, and what we're going to find is that the spouse who dies first is going to leave his/her wealth in a trust for the *use* and *benefit* of the surviving spouse. By "hiding" this spouse's wealth in a trust for the use and benefit of the surviving spouse, we are going to completely eliminate estate taxes. Here's how it works in more detail.

Let's look back at our married couple who had $1.1 million of net family wealth. What they do is, with legal assistance, divide that wealth between husband and wife. The husband can end up owning, in his name alone, $550,000 of wealth, and the wife can end up owning her own separate assets worth $550,000. In other words, some of the stocks go to the husband; some go to the wife. Part of the house goes to the husband; part of the house goes to the wife. Part of each asset goes to one spouse; the other part goes to the other spouse. (This kind of splitting is most easily done in the nine community property states, where all money earned during marriage, and all assets bought with that money, is, by state law, owned equally by each spouse.) Alternatively, you can shift entire blocks of assets to one spouse or the other: The husband ends up with all the stocks; the wife ends up with the house; the husband ends up with most of the cash; the wife ends up with all of the money market certificates. The key is to separate the wealth, part in the husband's name, and part in the wife's name. We do not want any major asset to be held as joint tenant with rights of survivorship, or as tenant by the entirety. (You'll see why very shortly.)

Having separated the wealth, the husband can prepare a will that says: "At my death, I want my $550,000 of wealth (or whatever amount it is when I die) to go into a trust for the use and benefit of my wife. She can be the trustee. She can use this wealth for her health, education, and ordinary and usual living expenses. She can use the income or the principal. When she dies, this trust will end, and the $550,000 of wealth (or whatever amount is then remaining) will go to the three children, equally."

When the husband dies, he has $550,000 of wealth. His estate will not pay any taxes, because of his $600,000 exemption.

Before we look back and examine in greater detail this trust that the husband has set up, let's take a quick look ahead and see what happens when the wife dies. Remember, during her remaining lifetime, she has been given the use and benefit from the husband's trust, which has $550,000 in it. Nevertheless, when she dies later on, she will not be taxed on the husband's $550,000. It was established and set up in a trust, and that trust will bypass taxation at her later death. The only assets that *will* be taxable at her death are her own $550,000. But because that amount is below the $600,000 exemption, the children will not pay any taxes. Therefore, by use of the husband's trust (called a *bypass trust* because it allows the husband's estate to bypass taxes when the wife dies later on), the parents have managed to leave $1.1 million to the children, completely free of federal estate tax. Compare this result to the clumsier result we had above, when the husband simply left everything he had to the wife, and that resulted in a $200,000 tax for the children when the wife eventually died. We have saved the children $200,000 in federal estate taxes!

Now let's look in more detail at the bypass trust that the husband sets up for the wife. Incidentally, the wife should and would have the identical provisions in her will or trust in case she were to die first and the husband were the survivor. In fact it's because we don't know whether the husband or wife is going to die first that we split the estate pretty much down the middle. If both estates are roughly the same size, then it really doesn't make any difference (taxwise) who dies first.

The husband's $550,000 will *not* go to the wife when he dies. Instead, it will go to a bypass trust. What rights can the wife get out of this bypass trust? First of all, she can be the sole trustee of this bypass trust. That means she does not have to go to any other person or institution to ask for money out of the trust. She can make all the investment decisions herself; she can buy, trade, or sell the assets within the trust at her own discretion. While it's true that in most states she will have to give an annual accounting of her transactions with respect to the trust to the ultimate beneficiaries (the children), and while it's true that they could squawk with respect to her investments or her use of the trust money, chances are they won't squawk too loudly, because she has a substantial club over them. Her own $550,000, which she controls by her will, can be left to any person or persons that she wishes. She can, therefore, cut out any one of her children who gives her a hard time with respect to her use of her late husband's bypass trust.

The wife can, as we've seen just above, be the sole trustee of the husband's bypass trust. As the trustee, she can shift the assets around. For example, if one of the assets that comprises the husband's $550,000 happened to be a condominium apartment, or part of the home, or some stocks, she could certainly sell those assets and use the money to purchase a new asset, such as a new condominium apartment, a new home, or a new investment. The new purchase would have to be registered in the name of the husband's trust because it's trust money that bought it; anyway, we sure don't want to put it in the wife's name, because that would increase her own estate.

What rights does the wife have as a *beneficiary* to her husband's trust? In other words, can she take out money from this trust for herself? And, if so, under what circumstances? The answer is that the wife can have all of the following rights as a beneficiary without jeopardizing the tax-free status of her husband's bypass trust. Incidentally, the husband could have his trust written to give her fewer rights than the following, since it's *his* trust; he just can't give her more rights or they'll lose their tax benefits.

She can receive all the income
that the trust generates

The trustee (whether it is the wife or someone else) will be investing part or all of the husband's $550,000. Any income those investments make can be distributed to the wife. In other words, she can be the sole beneficiary of the income from this trust. Alternatively, the husband could allow the children and the wife to be beneficiaries, in equal shares, or he could give the trustee discretion to distribute income to them in unequal shares. This kind of a provision would be particularly useful if the children needed some income as they were growing up.

She can receive as much principal as she needs,
but only for limited purposes

The wife can also withdraw principal, meaning the $550,000 itself, but only for limited purposes. The wife is allowed to use principal for her health, education, maintenance, and support (these last two words mean her ordinary and usual living expenses) to keep her at the same standard of living that she enjoyed while her husband was alive. She can withdraw limitless amounts of the trust principal for these four purposes.

Additionally, if someone else is the trustee, then that someone else can be authorized to review the wife's needs and distribute to her additional amounts of principal for things such as "comfort," "reasonable luxuries," "travel," and so on, the idea being that the independent trustee would be authorized to distribute amounts of principal to the wife for these "frivolities and luxuries," but that the wife would not be able to *demand* principal for these things. If the wife is her own trustee over this trust, however, she cannot be allowed the use of principal for any of these luxury-type items. She has to stay with "health, education, maintenance and support."

Of course, the husband does not need to make the wife the sole beneficiary of principal of his trust. He could provide, if he wanted, that the trustee (who could be the wife) could distribute principal to "my wife and children, in whatever amounts the trustee feels is necessary for their education, health, maintenance, and support." If the husband takes this more flexible approach, then the principal of his bypass trust can be used for his children after he has died. But again, it would be up to the trustee to decide how much principal to sprinkle among the wife and children, and if the wife is the trustee, that puts her in the driver's seat. (One small aside: The wife should be prohibited from using principal to take care of her legal obligations to raise any of the children. Most states require a parent to provide for the maintenance, support, health, and at least some of the education of a child while the child is a minor and maybe even thereafter. If the wife has the authority to use trust principal for these things, then, whether she in fact uses it or not for the children, the bypass trust will be taxable upon her later death. Therefore, it's a good idea to simply state that the wife cannot use the principal from the husband's trust to supplant any of the wife's legal obligations toward her children.)

She can receive a luxury amount
If the husband wishes, he can give his wife (or any other person or persons) an additional right to withdraw principal each year from the trust in an amount not greater than the

greater of $5,000 or 5 percent of the trust's principal. If the husband's trust is $550,000, this would give the wife the right to withdraw $27,500. If she does, the principal will be reduced, so the next year her 5 percent is worth less, but it would still be worth something! This is the amount she can use to go to Paris, buy a fur coat, and otherwise "live it up" now that the old boy has passed on. Incidentally, the right is noncumulative, so if it's not exercised in a calendar year, it can't be rolled over and added on to another "5 or 5" right the following year. And finally, this withdrawal right is completely optional, and the husband does not need to give it to his wife.

She can take a second look at the children

When the husband has his trust drawn up, he'll be asked by the attorney, "After you and your wife both die, how should your $550,000—or whatever is left of it after your wife's principal withdrawals—be divided up among the children?" The husband might answer, "Equally," and that provision would be put into his trust. However, after he has died and while the wife continues to live, the children's needs may change dramatically, so that an equal distribution on the wife's later death wouldn't be wise or what he would have wanted if he were still around. To avoid this he can, if he wants, give his wife the right to change the shares among the children, to change the time when each gets his or her share, or even to delete the kids and substitute the grandkids. This will give the wife a "club" over the children: "If you don't treat me nice, I'll change Dad's trust." But the club could end up bashing Dad in his grave if the wife abuses this power to "write out" Dad's favorite child, or to vindictively leave it all to the grandchildren. If the husband is worried that the power might be abused, especially as the wife gets older and possibly crotchety and disoriented, he shouldn't include it.

Review

Let's review for half a second. The husband and wife had more than $600,000 in net family wealth. They realized that if they left everything to the survivor of them, there would be a substantial tax when the survivor died and the estate went to the children. To avoid this, they divided their assets: the husband took some; the wife took the others. Each provided for a bypass trust to hold his/her assets upon death. The surviving spouse could be trustee of the bypass trust; could get all the income; could get principal for health, education, maintenance, and support; and could additionally take 5 percent or $5,000 of the principal every year. Upon the surviving spouse's later death, if the bypass trust complies with these rules, it will not be taxable in the surviving spouse's estate no matter what value it had, and would pass, completely tax free, to the children.

What about that dreaded new spouse? If the wife remarries, can her new husband have anything out of her late husband's bypass trust? The answer is no: That trust is only for the wife and, after her death, for the husband's children (or other named persons), and no money can be diverted to the wife's new husband. The monitors for this will be the children (or other ultimate beneficiaries), who can ask the wife for an annual accounting of the husband's trust. (Of course, the wife has her own $550,000, which is under her exclusive control, and she can leave that to her new husband if she so wishes. She would probably be better advised, however, to leave that in a bypass trust for her new husband's use during the remainder of his life, and then at his death, whatever remained unused would go back to her children. That way, she's taking care of her new spouse and also the children.)

We have, therefore, beaten the tax man for a married couple's estate of up to $1.2 million. Do you see why $1.2 million is the most that a married couple can use these bypass trusts for? The answer is that when the first spouse dies, the most that he/she can leave in his/her bypass trust is $600,000, because that's the most exemption that he/she will get. The most that the surviving spouse can leave the children is her/his own $600,000. Both of those add up to $1.2 million.

There is one final problem before moving on to estates over $1.2 million. That problem has to do with probate. (Remember probate?) When we separated out the assets so that the husband would have his own $600,000, or less, and the wife would have her own $600,000, or less, we inadvertently created a probate problem. That is because we want the assets of the spouse who dies first to be able to go into the bypass trust rather than to the surviving spouse. (That's why we can't allow joint tenancy or tenancy by the entirety on any valuable asset.) The only way we can be assured of enough control to get those assets into a bypass trust is by having the assets in the name of the spouse who dies first, so that he/she can then leave it under his/her will into a bypass trust. However, while this will solve the *tax* problem, since the assets are left in the sole name of the spouse, they will have to go through probate in order to get into the testamentary bypass trust.

A better solution, and one that is frequently employed,

is, after the assets are split, for the husband to establish his own (self-trusteed) living trust, and put his assets into it, and for the wife to establish her own separate (self-trusteed) living trust, and put her assets into it.

When the first spouse dies, there would be no probate (because of the living trust), and there would be no taxes (because the trust's assets are less than $600,000). When the surviving spouse dies, there's no probate or taxes on her/his own living trust for the same reasons, nor is there any probate or taxes on the first spouse's trust. The kids pay nothing to inherit up to $1.2 million! Let's hope it makes them humble.

EXAMPLE: Here's an example of a wife's living trust that "does it all." (Her husband's living trust would be a mirror image of this, except wherever her name appears, his name would appear, and vice versa.)

Minerva Married Revocable Living Trust

I, MINERVA MARRIED, hereby establish this revocable living trust, naming myself as trustee.

This trust shall be revocable and amendable by me at any time during my lifetime.

While I am alive, the income and principal of this trust shall be distributed to me as I direct. If I become incompetent, my successor trustee (named below) shall use the trust principal and income for my best interests.

When I die, the assets in this trust will avoid probate (because a living trust's assets avoid probate), and since the assets will not be over

$600,000, there will be no federal estate tax. I direct my successor trustee (named below) to hold the trust's assets under the following terms: Pay all of the income to my husband, for the rest of his life. The trustee can scatter the principal among my husband and three children for their health, education, maintenance, and support, without being required to keep the payments equal or pro rated. In making principal distributions, the trustee must take into consideration other assets readily available to each beneficiary for these purposes.

Additionally, my husband shall have the right to withdraw the greater of 5% of the trust amount, or $5,000, every calendar year.

After my husband and I have both died, this trust will again avoid probate (because living trust assets avoid probate), and will also escape estate taxation (because we have followed the rules of the bypass trust). My successor trustee (named below) will then take the remaining trust assets and distribute them as follows: 40% to child A, 50% to child B, and 10% to child C. If any of the children is then deceased, his or her share shall not go to his or her issue, but instead shall augment, proportionately, the shares of my remaining living children. These percentage shares may be altered by my husband after my death if he sees different needs develop as time goes by, but he may not leave less than 10% to any child.

The successor trustees of this trust are as follows: first, my husband; and when he for any reason ceases to act, then XYZ Trust Company.

The powers of the trustee are as follows: [You probably have the idea by now that it's a good idea to give the trustee very broad powers for investments, so we won't bother to go through them again.]

Dated: _____   _____

                         MINERVA MARRIED,
                         Settlor

                         _____

                         MINERVA MARRIED,
                         Trustee

Here is a schematic diagram of how this married couple has set up their living trusts, bypass trusts, and estate.

MIKE	MINERVA
$550,000, held in self-trusteed living trust	$550,000, held in self-trusteed living trust
↓	
Mike dies. No probate or estate taxes. Minerva becomes successor trustee.	
↓	↓
Minerva dies. No probate or estate taxes. XYZ becomes successor trustee and distributes estate to children.	Minerva dies. No probate or estate taxes. XYZ becomes successor trustee and distributes estate to children.

See how easy it is? You take a few simple precautions, and you hold the tax and probate bogeymen at bay.

· · ·

For Married Couples with Net Family Wealth of Over $1.2 Million

If you add up your total worth and determine that the amount you could leave would be in excess of $1.2 million if you and your spouse were both to die, then there are a number of considerations that will apply to you. First, in order to shelter the first $1.2 million of your wealth from federal estate tax, you are probably going to want to use bypass trusts, as discussed in the previous section. However, because your estate exceeds this limit there is going to be a tax on the excess unless you utilize some estate planning techniques in addition to the bypass trust. Those techniques are discussed below, but before we get to them, let's look at how the excess over $1.2 million can be treated when the first one of you dies.

EXAMPLE: The husband and wife add up their net family wealth and determine that they have $2 million of assets that they are able to leave the children after they have both died. In order to avoid probate, the husband sets up a revocable living trust and names himself as trustee; the wife does the same, naming herself as trustee. They know that each trust must have bypass provisions for $600,000 per trust; that will pass $1.2 million free of federal estate taxes to the children. Each therefore provides in his/her trust that upon his/her death, his/her trust will hold $600,000 under bypass provisions we've already learned about. The husband then segregates $600,000 of assets, and funds his trust with this amount; the wife segregates an additional $600,000 of assets, and funds her trust with those assets. They have now succeeded in (1) avoiding federal estate taxes on $1.2 million (because of the bypass provisions of each trust) and (2) avoiding probate on the $1.2 million (because it's held in living trusts).

What about the last $800,000 of net family wealth? This can be put into the husband's revocable living trust, into the wife's revocable living trust, or divided between the two trusts. (It's a good idea to put it into one trust or the other, or both, in order to avoid probate on it.)

Let's assume that, for this example, the husband takes $500,000 of that excess wealth and puts it in his living trust, and the wife takes the remaining $300,000 and puts it in her living trust.

If the husband dies first, his trust will be worth $1.1 million. We know that the most he can hold in the bypass provisions of his trust is $600,000, so that leaves him with $500,000 that he has to do something with. His alternatives are these: (1) give it to his wife and get a complete marital deduction, thereby paying no tax; (2) give it to his bypass trust or to the children, but since he's already used up his $600,000 exemption, there would be a tax payable if he were to do either of these things; (3) put it into a subtrust for the wife's use and benefit, which would not be a bypass trust (since he's used up all of the $600,000 exemption), but another kind that would qualify for the marital deduction.

Here's a diagram of these three options.

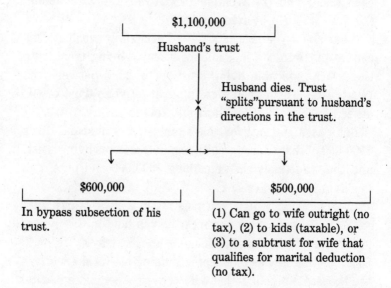

$1,100,000

Husband's trust

Husband dies. Trust "splits"pursuant to husband's directions in the trust.

$600,000

In bypass subsection of his trust.

$500,000

(1) Can go to wife outright (no tax), (2) to kids (taxable), or (3) to a subtrust for wife that qualifies for marital deduction (no tax).

Of these three options, most people pick either the first or the third; few people wish to pay any tax until they absolutely have to. Therefore, if the husband gives his $500,000 to his wife, or channels it into a subtrust for her use and benefit that would qualify for the marital deduction, he is postponing the tax on this $500,000 until his wife's later death. She'll be taxed on it later (unless she spends it during her remaining lifetime), since she'll have, at her death, her own $900,000 plus this $500,000, or $800,000 more than the $600,000 she can leave free of estate tax.

The husband can certainly have the $500,000 transferred outright to his wife at his death (the first option). This would avoid federal estate taxes because of the unlimited marital deduction, but the problem is that the money would then be available for the wife's disposal in any way she saw fit. She might get remarried and leave it all to her new husband. Alternatively, she could leave it to a favorite child, and cut the others out. She could leave it to a favorite charity. In short, she can give it to anybody she wants, since it will be her money. If the husband is not happy with this, he should not give the $500,000 outright to his wife at his death, but instead should leave it in a subtrust that qualifies for the unlimited marital deduction (the third option).

There are two kinds of subtrusts that will qualify for the unlimited marital deduction, thereby relieving this $500,000 from any federal estate tax when the husband dies. Under the first kind of subtrust, the husband must provide that the wife receives all the income from the $500,000 for the rest of her life, payable at least annually. He can also allow her to use the principal, but this is optional with him. Upon her death, she must be given the right to state, in her will, who gets the $500,000 in the subtrust. Clearly, this kind of subtrust is objectionable for the same reasons that an outright gift to the wife is objectionable: She can leave the $500,000, at her death, to *anyone* she wants, including a new husband, favorite child, charity, etc., meaning the husband has completely lost control over it.

The second kind of subtrust that the husband could put this $500,000 in is called a *QTIP trust*. Under this kind of trust, the wife must be given all the net income that the subtrust earns for the rest of her life, payable at least annually. He can also allow her to use the principal if he wants to. However, at her death, she does *not* have the right to determine who gets the $500,000. Instead, the $500,000 will go to whomever the husband has designated in his QTIP subtrust. In other words, with a QTIP subtrust, the wife

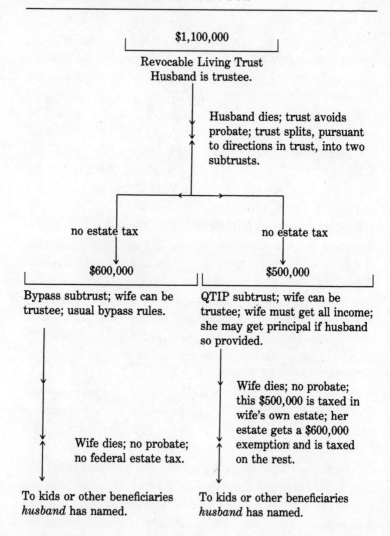

$1,100,000

Revocable Living Trust
Husband is trustee.

Husband dies; trust avoids probate; trust splits, pursuant to directions in trust, into two subtrusts.

no estate tax

no estate tax

$600,000

$500,000

Bypass subtrust; wife can be trustee; usual bypass rules.

QTIP subtrust; wife can be trustee; wife must get all income; she may get principal if husband so provided.

Wife dies; no probate; this $500,000 is taxed in wife's own estate; her estate gets a $600,000 exemption and is taxed on the rest.

Wife dies; no probate; no federal estate tax.

To kids or other beneficiaries *husband* has named.

To kids or other beneficiaries *husband* has named.

has the use of the income from the subtrust during her remaining lifetime, and at her death, the assets will end up going to whomever the *husband* (and not the wife) has designated.

QTIP subtrusts are becoming enormously popular among married couples because each spouse then has ultimate control over where her/his assets are distributed after both spouses have died.

If this is confusing, look at the schematic diagram on page 110 of how the husband's revocable living trust would, at his death, split into a bypass subtrust and a QTIP subtrust.

In Summary

If you are married and your net family wealth exceeds $1.2 million, then you are probably going to want to use bypass trusts to insulate the first $1.2 million from estate taxes. Any amount over $1.2 million will be taxable but, if you do it correctly, only when the surviving spouse has died. When the first spouse dies, $600,000 of wealth will be retained in a bypass trust for the use and benefit of the surviving spouse, and any other wealth that the deceased spouse owned will be either (1) given outright to the surviving spouse; (2) put in a trust for the surviving spouse where the surviving spouse has the right to direct the ultimate disposition of the trust principal when she/he dies later on; or (3) put into a QTIP trust, where the surviving spouse does *not* have the right to direct where the trust principal goes when she/he dies later on.

But note now that we've thus far only discussed *postponing* the tax on amounts over $1.2 million. Suppose instead you want to *eliminate* the tax on that excess. How do you do it? Let's now look at some ways that can be used to reduce or eliminate those taxes for married couples whose net family wealth is in excess of $1.2 million, and for single people whose net wealth is in excess of $600,000.

Estate Reduction Techniques for Single People Whose Net Wealth Exceeds $600,000, and for Married Couples Whose Net Family Wealth Exceeds $1.2 Million

There are a number of techniques that can be used to eliminate federal estate taxes completely, no matter what size your estate is. Remember, if you're single, we only have to make the excess over $600,000 disappear; if you're married and use bypass trusts, we need to reduce your estate to $1.2 million. We'll start with the easy techniques and move on to the more sophisticated and complicated ones. You should know, at the outset, that some of these techniques are not greeted with open arms by the IRS, and before you embark on any of them, you should definitely seek a tax specialist for assistance.

Outright gifts of $10,000 per recipient per year
As you know from page 57, every calendar year you can give $10,000 worth of assets to each of as many different people as you wish. If you keep each recipient's gift at or below $10,000, you pay no federal gift tax. And, no matter how big the gift, the recipient does not have to pay gift or income taxes on it. The assets need not be cash; they can be stocks, bonds, diamonds, interests in real estate, automobiles, or anything else. The recipient of your gift need not be a family member; he or she can be any person at all. If your gift is $10,000 or less in a calendar year, then you need not report it to the Internal Revenue Service at all; if it exceeds $10,000, then it must be reported on a gift tax return to the IRS, and any amount in excess of $10,000 will use up part of your $600,000 death-time credit.

EXAMPLE: Sally Single makes a $9,000 gift to her daughter, and a $15,000 gift to her next-door neighbor. The gift to her daughter is not even reported to the IRS, as it's below the annual gift tax exemption. However, as to the neighbor's gift: $10,000 is exempt from gift taxes; the last $5,000 of the gift is reportable to the Internal Revenue Service on a gift tax return. Rather than actually pay a tax on that $5,000, Sally *must*, under the law, use up $5,000 of her $600,000 death-time exemption. That means that when she dies, she will only be allowed to leave $595,000 free of federal estate tax.

This example shows you that the gift taxes and the estate taxes are unified, meaning if you give over $10,000 per recipient, then you just reduce your death-time exemption. Thus, to reduce a big estate, you can't do it all at once unless you have a lot of donees.

EXAMPLE: Sally Single has an estate of $800,000, and two donees she really cares about. She can avoid reducing her $600,000 death-time exemption only by giving her excess $200,000 away in $10,000 per year gifts to each of her two donees.

If you are married, your spouse can authorize you to use her/his $10,000 exemption, so that with this permission, you can give $20,000 worth of assets to a donee in any calendar year.

If you have a choice of things to give, it might be better to give away an asset that is likely to appreciate (such as a stock, or an interest in a piece of real estate) rather than an asset that is not likely to appreciate (such as cash). The reason for this is obvious: If you hold on to the appreciating asset, then its value, as of your date of death, will be taxed in your estate. But if you were to give that appreciating asset away, then the asset as well as its future appreciation will be out of your control and hence out of your taxable estate.

The final point about making outright gifts has nothing to do with saving federal *estate* taxes, but has to do with reducing *income* taxes. Once you give an asset away, any income or dividend or interest that it might earn will be taxable to the donee of the gift, and not to you. However, under the new "flat tax" law recently passed, if you give an asset to your child who is under fourteen, then any income in excess of $1,000 per year that the asset earns will be taxable to the child not at the child's (lower) income tax bracket, but instead at your (higher) income tax bracket. Once the child is fourteen years of age or over, then the income the asset earns will be taxed to the child at his or her own income tax rate, and not at yours.

Outright gifts are a mixed blessing. The benefit is obvious: If you and your spouse have three children, three sons- and daughters-in-law, and four grandchildren, that means you have a total of ten potential recipients, each of whom you can give $20,000 per year. That means $200,000 per year could be removed from your taxable estate; when you die, that $200,000 will not be subject to federal estate taxes at all. And you can give this amount of money away every year, year in and year out, right up to the moment you die. You can see that after a very short period of time, you can substantially reduce your taxable estate, perhaps even getting it down to the $1.2 million level if you're married, or the $600,000 level if you're single.

The problem with outright gifts is that they are outright gifts. You lose control of the asset, and you may lose control of the donee! Once the asset is out of your control, it's probably gone for good, and you shouldn't count on the donee "giving it back" if you should ever need it. Many parents are quite concerned that their wealth will not be enough to support them if they should become seriously ill or have to go to a nursing home for an extended period of time. If you are concerned about this, then the best advice might be to be exceedingly careful about giving anything away; after all, it doesn't make much sense to cramp your own life-style solely to benefit your heirs.

Let's now have a look at a technique that (1) reduces your taxable estate and (2) needn't mean the loss of substantial assets out of your pocket while you are living. This has to do with life insurance.

Transfer of life insurance

You may have been surprised, in reading this book, to learn that life insurance proceeds form part of your estate and are taxable when you die. Most people mistakenly believe that life insurance is not taxable when they die. It does avoid probate and (like any other asset received from a dead person) income taxes, but it usually doesn't avoid *estate* taxes. Actually, life insurance can be made nontaxable when you die, but it takes a little bit of doing.

First, the rules. Life insurance is taxable in your estate if (1) its beneficiary is your estate or (2) you are the insured and the owner of the policy. To avoid the first rule, simply never have your estate as your beneficiary; instead, name a person, trust, charity, etc. The second rule is tougher to understand and beat. You need three definitions to make some headway here.

INSURED: This is the person whose life is insured, and who must die before any money is paid by the life insurance company.

BENEFICIARY: This is the person who receives the money from the life insurance company when the insured dies.

OWNER: This is the person who has one or more rights in the life insurance policy. For example, the owner could have the right to change the beneficiary, the right to borrow money against the policy, the right to use the policy as collateral for a loan, and/or the right to change the kind of policy from one type to another (for example, from whole life to term, or vice versa). Usually, the insured is the owner of the policy on the insured's life.

The rule is this: If you are the insured and also the owner, then the proceeds of your life insurance policy will be included in your estate for tax purposes when you die, no matter who the beneficiary is.

EXAMPLE: A father is the insured on a $500,000 policy. He also has the right to change the beneficiary, so he is the owner (he may also have other ownership rights, but the law is that if you have any single ownership right at all, then you are deemed to be the owner). Therefore, when the father dies, the $500,000 will go to the beneficiary, but the $500,000 will count in the father's taxable estate.

Since life insurance proceeds usually constitute a major portion of a person's estate, and since life insurance policies are usually worth very little to the insured while he or she is living, life insurance policies make an ideal asset to give away. If you give away the ownership rights, so that the "insured" is not the "owner", then nice tax results occur.

EXAMPLE: A father has a $500,000 policy on which he is both the owner and the insured. He cannot change the fact that he is the insured party, but he can give the ownership rights to the beneficiary. If his daughter is the beneficiary, he can give the ownership rights away to her. The law says that he must live three years from the time he gives the ownership rights in the policy away to his daughter; if he lives those three years and then dies, the daughter will receive the proceeds of the policy (as beneficiary), but the policy will not be taxed in the father's estate. In other words, by having transferred the ownership of the policy and living three years, the father has eliminated the policy from his estate, and the daughter gets the proceeds tax free. Remember that if the father's estate exclusive of the life insurance is over $600,000 (single) or $1.2 million (if he's married and he and his wife used bypass trusts), the excess will be taxed at forty cents on the dollar. This father, then, by reducing his estate by $500,000, has saved his daughter $200,000.

If the owner of the policy is not the insured, as in the example immediately above, then the owner must be sure to name himself or herself as the beneficiary. As in the example above, the owner (the daughter) must be sure to name herself as the beneficiary; if she names someone else as the beneficiary (let's say her child), then when the insured person dies, the owner will be deemed to have made a taxable gift to the beneficiary (her child).

How can we use this technique of separation of "insured" and "owner"? For single people, the ownership of the life insurance policy could be transferred immediately to the beneficiary of the policy, as in the example just above. But if you believe that your beneficiary is too young or immature to handle the life insurance proceeds, then you can transfer the ownership of the policy to an irrevocable trust, which, upon your death, would receive the proceeds of the policy and hold them for the beneficiary until the beneficiary has attained a more mature age. The trust must be irrevocable when you establish it, and you must have no right to revoke it, change it, amend it, or do anything else with it or with the policy.

How do married couples use this technique?

EXAMPLE: The husband is insured for $200,000 through his group term policy provided by his employer. Since the husband has the right to change the beneficiary of the policy, he is deemed to be the owner. Therefore, he is both the insured and owner, so the $200,000 will form part of his taxable estate when he dies. If he names his wife as beneficiary, then there would be no tax on the $200,000 when he dies, because of the unlimited marital deduction. However, that $200,000 would then form part of the wife's estate later on when she dies (to the extent she has not spent it during her remaining lifetime), and if she is wealthy enough to have her own estate of $600,000 or more, then that $200,000 is going to be taxed before it reaches the children, or whomever she leaves it to under her will or trust.

Therefore, for married couples where the surviving spouse's estate will be $600,000 or more, it does not make any sense to just leave the life insurance to your surviving spouse, because it will simply be fully taxed after you've both died.

Likewise, you're not gaining anything by naming your spouse as the owner of the policy on your life. All that technique does is remove the policy from your estate if you live three years; but if you had named your spouse as beneficiary, and kept the ownership yourself, the proceeds would have been excluded under the marital deduction. Either way, your spouse receives the insurance tax-free, but that insurance inflates her/his taxable estate later on at her/his death.

What do married couples do with large policies? Certainly the husband could give the ownership of the policy to the children. If he did so, they would be the owners, and he would be the insured. If he lived three years, the policy would be out of his estate. The problem with this technique is that the wife would then not receive any benefits from the $200,000 during her remaining lifetime, since the children had to name themselves as beneficiaries in order to avoid the taxable gift result had they named someone else as beneficiary.

Is there any way that we can (1) get the policy out of the husband's taxable estate, (2) provide for the wife during her remaining lifetime with the policy proceeds, and (3) provide that when the wife dies, none of the policy will be taxable in her estate? The answer is that all three of these goals can be attained by the use of an irrevocable bypass trust.

EXAMPLE: The husband is insured for $200,000. He is also the owner. He establishes an irrevocable bypass trust and transfers the ownership rights to the trust so that the trust is the owner of his policy. The trustee (the new owner) then names the trust as the beneficiary of the policy. The husband lives three years, and then dies. None of the $200,000 is taxable in the husband's estate. The $200,000 is paid to the trust because the trust is the beneficiary. The trustee then uses the $200,000 for the wife's benefit, under the terms of a standard bypass trust, which we have previously explored in greater detail. The wife can receive all of the income from the trust; she can receive principal for her needs; and yet when she dies, none of the remaining principal of the trust would be taxable in her estate. It can then be held for the children until they reach a more mature age, or distributed to them if they are mature already; whichever the husband wanted would be specified in the trust.

This is a terrific deal! You don't get taxed on the policy at your death; your spouse gets the use of the insurance money for the rest of her/his life; it's not taxed when your spouse dies; and it goes to the kids completely tax-free. No estate tax, ever!

The disadvantages to transferring the ownership rights in a policy to another person or to an irrevocable trust should be obvious: You, the insured, lose all of the ownership rights, such as the right to change the beneficiary, the right to borrow against the policy, the right to use it as collateral for a loan, and so on. Additionally, if you're going to use a trust as the owner, the trust must be irrevocable, meaning that you cannot change any of the trust terms. If you later get angry at your spouse, or at one of your children, or want to postpone the age at which the children receive their share of the life insurance money, you cannot do it, since the trust is irrevocable. But these detriments are pretty minor compared to the major benefit of having a huge chunk of wealth excluded from the tax man's reach.

Finally, there is a gift element hidden in all of this. When you transfer the ownership rights to the new owner, whether the new owner be a person or a trust, there is a possible hidden gift. This is because the ownership rights may have a value. If you are transferring the ownership rights on a term policy, the ownership rights will probably have very little value. However, if you are transferring the ownership rights on a whole life policy, or a universal life policy, it's conceivable that the ownership rights could have a substantial cash value, called the *cash surrender value*. A little precaution can solve this problem: You simply borrow against the policy before you make the transfer, so that at the time of the transfer, the ownership rights have very little value, meaning that the gift has very little or no value.

Who continues to pay the premiums after you transfer the ownership rights? Typically, the insured does, unless he or she can talk the new owner into paying them! Every time the insured pays the premium, the IRS takes the position that he or she is making a gift to the new owner of the policy.

Therefore, there are two times a gift can be made when ownership rights are transferred. First, when the old owner transfers the policy to the new owner; second, when the insured pays the premium for the new owner. If the new owner is a person, and not a trust, then it may be that the value of each gift is less than the $10,000 that can be gifted annually, free of gift tax.

EXAMPLE: A father, a widower, has $600,000 worth of cash, stocks, and home. Additionally, he is the insured and owner on a $300,000 life insurance policy that names his daughter, Jennie, as beneficiary. If he undertakes no tax avoidance, at his death his estate will be $900,000, minus his $600,000 exemption, leaving $300,000 taxable. The estate tax would be about $120,000 (.40 × $300,000). To avoid this huge tax, he transfers the ownership of the policy to Jennie. The policy's cash surrender value is $8,000, so he's made her an $8,000 gift, which is less than he's allowed to give her annually free of gift tax. Good ole Dad continues to pay the premiums ($2,000 per year), which again are less than the $10,000 he can give Jennie free of gift tax. Thus, there's no gift tax at all. If Dad lives three years from the date of transfer to Jennie, none of the $300,000 will be subject to estate tax in his estate, saving $120,000 in estate taxes!

If the new owner is an irrevocable trust, then the gift tax consequences get a little stranger. The Internal Revenue Service takes the position that, where the trust is the owner, people must be named in the trust to have the right to withdraw the value of the ownership rights and the premiums as they are paid by the insured. Consequently, the insured is going to want to name people, and give them this withdrawal right, who will have very little interest in withdrawing the premium after it is paid.

EXAMPLE: Mom and Dad have stock, cash, and real estate worth $1,100,000. To completely shelter this from estate taxes, they each establish living bypass trusts, and put $550,000 worth of wealth in each living trust. So far, so good. However, Mom is insured for $300,000 by her employer's group term policy, and she is the owner, since she can change the beneficiary. If she names Dad as the beneficiary and dies, there's no tax because of the marital deduction. However, Dad now has $850,000 in his estate (the

$300,000 life insurance money plus the $550,000 in his living trust), which is more than the $600,000 he can leave tax-free, so his estate will have to pay a tax. Foreseeing all this, Mom established an irrevocable bypass trust and transferred the life insurance into it. The value of the ownership rights are $800, and the annual premium is $1,500. The irrevocable trust names persons who can withdraw this money, so there's no gift tax. If Mom lives three years, there's no estate tax in her estate either. Dad will get benefits from the trust, and on his death there will be no estate taxes either (since it's a bypass trust), so the balance left in the trust can go to the kids or whomever, completely free of estate tax!

In Summary

Giving away cash or other assets can hurt, but where you give away life insurance, which usually has little lifetime value to you, it doesn't hurt as much. Add that to the fact that life insurance can be one of the largest assets in your taxable estate at your death, and you can see why giving away life insurance is a very popular tax-saving device.

To get reoriented for a moment; we're looking at ways to reduce your taxable estate down to $600,000 (single) or $1.2 million (married and use bypass trusts) so your heirs pay no estate tax at your death. The two techniques we just looked at (gifts and life insurance transfer) will probably be enough to bring many, if not most, estates down to the nontaxable limit, so most of you won't have to read further. However, if you're richer or just curious, let's move on.

Now we get into wonderland. The following techniques are "state of the art," and the IRS has not laid down, played dead, and agreed that they always work. If, after all the warnings in this book against "do-it-yourselfers," you still think you can do it on your own, *please don't*! The following discussions ought to dissuade you.

Sale of a Remainder Interest

This technique allows you to (1) keep an asset until you have died; (2) get an extra income during your life; (3) transfer all future appreciation in the asset to your children so that that appreciation won't be taxed in your estate; and (4) have the asset itself excluded from your taxable estate when you die. In other words, even though you had the use of an asset during your lifetime, it will disappear from your taxable estate when you die. What a deal!

EXAMPLE: Your business is worth $1 million. Your two children are working in it. You and your spouse have $1.2 million of other assets that are fully sheltered and eliminated from the federal estate tax by bypass trusts. Your business causes your estate to exceed $1.2 million, so it'll be taxed at 40 percent when the kids get it—a very unpleasant prospect. One solution (but not a good one) is to begin giving it away to the kids. If your spouse agrees to let you use her/his $10,000 exemption, you can give each child $20,000 per year. Assuming the business doesn't increase in value in the interim, it would take you twentyfive years to give it away. That's one problem; the other is that you'll eventually lose control. Is that a good idea? Remember King Lear? Let's try another approach to getting this business out of your taxable estate.

EXAMPLE: Your business is worth $1 million. Instead of trying to give it away, if you *sold* the business to the kids right now, you'd get $1 million, because that's what it's worth. There are two problems with this. First, an outright sale will not reduce your taxable estate a penny, since you're only exchanging a business for cash, and either will be valued and taxed at your death. Second, you don't *want* to sell it to the kids now, because you want to hold it until you die. So here's the deal: If you sell the kids the *right* to have the business *later on* when you die, lots of good things happen. (You might want to read that last sentence twice! Another way to look at this is that the kids are *buying* their inheritance from you.) First, you get to keep the business, the voting rights, and dividends until you die (a *life estate*), because all you've sold the children is the right to have those things later on when you die (the *remainder*). Second, the children, who are buying this inheritance from you, will begin paying you money right now in order to get it later on. This will increase your income and make it easier for you in your golden years. Third, when you die later on, the Internal Revenue Service should agree that *none* of the business will be in your taxable estate. Why? The answer is that you have nothing left to give anybody, and the federal estate tax is a tax upon things that you have the power to give away when you die. You don't have any part of the business to give away to anybody because you've already sold it to the children. Finally, even if the business appreciates during your remaining lifetime from the $1 million it is worth now to, say, $4 million at the time of your death, none of that $3 million appreciation is going to be taxable in your estate; instead, the children have bought the remainder in the business, and along with it goes any future appreciation.

How much are the children going to have to pay you to buy the remainder from you? (Incidentally, you can't gift them the remainder, because if you do, then a specific section of the Internal Revenue Code comes into play and the whole business will be taxable in your estate.) Remember that you are keeping the business until you die, and the kids are paying you *now* for the right to receive the business at that *later* point in time. Clearly, the younger you are, the longer they are going to have to wait, so the less they would have to pay you now; conversely, the older you are, it's more likely that they won't have to wait as long, so they should pay you more. Here are some examples from the table that the IRS uses to determine how much the children should pay you for the business.

YOUR AGE	VALUE OF YOUR LIFE ESTATE	VALUE OF REMAINDER
20	.97365	.02635
30	.95543	.04457
40	.91571	.08429
50	.84743	.15257
60	.74491	.25509
70	.60522	.39478
80	.43659	.56341
90	.28221	.71779

EXAMPLE: Assuming your business is worth $1 million and you are sixty years of age, the children would have to pay you $1,000,000 × .255090, or $255,090, right now for their *remainder interest*. Whether they pay you in a lump sum or in installments, when you die it's a bonanza for the kids: Your estate has in it only the $255,090, not the $1 million—a reduction of $744,010 in your estate, which means a $297,604 savings in federal estate tax ($744,010 × .40 = $297,604).

Another way of looking at this is that you keep the business until you die, which satisfies you; the kids' estate tax payment is reduced by $297,604; the only out-of-pocket cost to the kids is what they actually pay you of the $255,090, which, unless you spend it, they'll inherit back anyway.

A disadvantage to the children, in addition to having to pay you, is that whatever they pay you for the business will be their *basis* in the business, meaning that if they sell the business later on, the difference between what they sell it for and their basis will be their capital gain. If they don't sell it, however, then they needn't worry about their basis.

EXAMPLE: The children sell the business later on for $4 million, having bought it from you for $255,090. Their capital gain is $3,744,010; under the new flat tax law it would be taxable to the children either at 15 percent or 28 percent depending upon their other income and the terms of the sale. This rather large capital gain is to be contrasted with what would happen if you were not to have entered into this sale arrangement with your children, and instead died owning the asset.

EXAMPLE: Instead of selling the remainder interest in the business to the children for $255,090, you don't sell them anything. Instead, you hang on to the business until you die. In this case, the entire business will be appraised at your death, and subject to federal estate tax. Assuming that the business is worth $4 million when you die, and assuming that you had $600,000 of other assets to use up your $600,000 exemption, your $4 million business will attract a 40 percent federal estate tax at your death, or $1.6 million. However, when an asset goes through somebody's estate at death, it gathers a new basis, which would be the value of the asset as of date of death. In other words, after the children pay the $1.6 million in federal estate tax, they will receive the business with an adjusted basis of $4 million. If they turn around and sell the business for $4 million, there would be no capital gains at all.

This technique, called *sale of the remainder interest*, is therefore a double-edged sword if the children sell the asset later on. While the asset would escape the federal estate tax in your estate, it will attract a federal capital gains income tax later on if the children decide to sell the asset. That capital gains income tax can be eliminated or substantially reduced if the asset is subject to estate tax in your estate, but it's probable that the estate tax would be larger than the capital gains tax would be. In other words, you can beat one tax, but you can't beat them both. Which is better for you and your family situation? Check with your lawyer.

There are a few points to be made about this technique. The first is that it may not work for a sale of an asset that is not likely to earn an income. For example, there is some question as to whether this technique can be used for the sale of a painting, a beach house you don't rent, unimproved land, slow-growth stock, and so on.

EXAMPLE: Father has a painting by Picasso worth $3 million. Father is seventy-five years of age. Can Father sell the remainder interest in the Picasso to his children for $1, 435,530 ($3,000,000 × .47851)? If he can, then when he dies, the Picasso and all of its appreciation will be excluded from his estate. He'll have removed at least $3 million from his estate. In his estate will be the remaining balance on the promissory note from the children, the payments he has already received from them less the income tax he has paid on those payments, and the interest those payments have earned him while he was alive.

Now let's have some hard looks at the money the kids have to pay you. First, where are they going to get the money to pay right now for their remainder interest? As stated above, you can provide that the kids pay you over a number of years, in installments. This should assist them. Furthermore, if they're paying you in installments, you can make up your mind every year whether or not you want to forgive $10,000 (or if you're married, $20,000) of their indebtedness to you. In other words, you can gift back to them $10,000 or $20,000 every year. This will not enable you to escape the income tax you will have to pay as you receive your payments, but it will certainly assist in the children's cash flow problems.

Next, as we have seen in the examples above, when you die, the unpaid balance on the installment note *is* taxable in your estate (the asset itself—like the business or the painting—isn't, but the amount still owed you is). Is there any way that the unpaid balance on the note can be eliminated from your taxable estate, since it's likely to be one of the biggest items in your estate? The answer is that there are two separate techniques that can be used, *private an-*

nuity and *self-canceling installment note*, and these are discussed in the following two sections. Because these techniques can make the note "disappear," very few kids have any incentive to pay off Dad completely in one lump sum, choosing instead to delay payment as long as possible. Anyway, that lump sum, if invested by Dad, would just earn interest in his estate that would be taxed at his death.

A last word of caution. Since the children are purchasing part of the business (the remainder), the father has, to some extent, lost full control over the business. In other words, if he wants to sell, he's going to have to get his children's permission. In order to prevent any misunderstanding or disagreements about "who has the reins," when the sale of the remainder interest agreement is entered into between the father and the children, there should be further written understanding between the father and the children regarding (1) who makes the decision with respect to whether the business may be sold during the father's lifetime and (2) if the business is sold, whether the money is then divided between the father and the children, or whether the father can continue to receive interest from the entire pot of money, or whether the money may be reinvested in other assets, and if so, what rights the father and the children have in those new assets.

All of these problems aside, the sale of the remainder interest is a very exciting method of having your cake and eating it too, holding on to an asset for the rest of your life, getting an income you otherwise wouldn't get, and having that asset disappear from your taxable estate when you die. Clearly, this technique needs some expert advise, so don't try to blunder through it on your own, or you may blunder right into the arms of the IRS.

Now let's look at two techniques that can be used separately, by themselves, or can be used along with a sale of a remainder interest, both of which operate when an asset is sold, and which provide that any unpaid amounts on the indebtedness back to you will be canceled and not subject to estate tax when you die.

Sale by Means of a Private Annuity

We've just seen that if you sell an asset while you are alive and receive a lump sum payment back, when you die, that lump sum payment, plus all interest or other earnings it has generated during your remaining lifetime, will be in your taxable estate.

EXAMPLE: You sell your vacation home to a third party for $200,000. You are paid off in a lump sum of $200,000, and pay your income tax on the gain (if any) in the sale of the house. You then invest the remainder of the lump sum in money market certificates, treasury bills, stocks, bonds, etc. When you die, those assets, plus the net income they have generated during your remaining lifetime, will be part of your taxable estate.

Recognizing this, some people have attempted to "sell" an asset for less than its fair market value. Usually this "sale" is to a close relative, who benefits by paying far less than the asset is actually worth. From a tax perspective, what is really going on here is a disguised gift.

EXAMPLE: Dad "sells" his vacation home to his daughter for $5,000; the actual fair market value of the vacation home is $200,000. Dad has made a gift to his daughter of $195,000;

Dad is obligated to file a federal gift tax return, showing a gift of $195,000. Ten thousand dollars of that gift can be free of gift tax (assuming Dad has made no other gifts to his daughter during that calendar year); the other $185,000 of gift will use up $185,000 of Dad's $600,000 exemption. Therefore, when Dad dies, he will not be allowed to leave $600,000 free of federal estate tax; he will be allowed to leave only $415,000 free of estate tax.

As we learned in the preceding section, if you sell an asset and instead of taking a lump sum payment agree with the buyer to take your payment in installments, when you die, any unpaid balance still due to you is included in your taxable estate. However, there are two techniques that can be used to make that unpaid balance disappear from your taxable estate. The first is called a *private annuity*; the second is called a *self-canceling installment note*. (Incidentally, a simple direction in your will that "I forgive all debts" or "I forgive the balance owing to me from my daughter in the promissory note whereby she bought the summer home" will *not* exclude the debt from your taxable estate.)

A *private annuity* is a technique whereby you sell an asset and the buyer promises to pay you back the purchase price in set dollar amounts over the rest of your life. The benefit to this is that when you die, no more payments are due, and none of the balance owing is in your taxable estate.

EXAMPLE: A father sells a beach house to his daughter for $200,000, its fair market value. Using the table we'll review shortly, the father and daughter determine that the daughter will pay the $200,000 in annual installments of $20,000, payable each year for as long as the father lives. *If* the father dies in the second year after the sale, then

$40,000 (less any income taxes paid) would be included in his estate (which is the amount he had received from his daughter), and no further amount would be included in his estate. In other words, he has managed to transfer a $200,000 vacation home to his daughter, while his estate only has to pay estate taxes on the amount received, $40,000. (Of course, if Dad has spent that $40,000, then it would not be in his estate; on the other side of the coin, if he has invested that $40,000, then the money plus interest earned would be in his estate.)

Notice that not only is the asset itself (the beach house) removed from Dad's taxable estate when he dies (because he had sold it and didn't own it anymore), but also its appreciation is removed from his estate as well. If, for example, the beach house had appreciated to $300,000 by the time he died, then had he not sold it to his daughter, the $300,000 value of the house would be included in his estate. But because the asset was sold, the extra $100,000 of appreciation is not taxed in Dad's estate, but instead accrues to the daughter. In this instance, the daughter has made an even better deal: She has received a $300,000 asset for a total purchase price of $40,000; the difference, $260,000, has been effectively eliminated from Dad's taxable estate.

This technique can backfire. The seller must be paid the annual installment annuity amount for *each year until he dies*. If the seller lives beyond his or her life expectancy, then the buyer must nevertheless continue paying the seller the annual annuity amounts. Therefore, if you outlive your life expectancy, the buyer is going to overpay you for what he or she bought—an inducement to homicide. Yours.

How much will the buyer have to pay annually? The answer is that it depends on what the seller's life expectancy is and the fair market value of the asset. Simply determine how old the seller is, and find the appropriate annuity factor from the examples in the table below, which is used by the IRS; then divide the present fair market value of the asset by the annuity factor.

AGE OF SELLER	ANNUITY FACTOR
50	8.4743
55	8.0046
60	7.4491
65	6.7970
70	6.0522
75	5.2149
80	4.3659

EXAMPLE: Father, who is fifty, sells an asset worth $200,000 to his son. The annuity amount, which the son will have to pay to his father every year until the father dies, is $23,601 per year. This is determined by dividing the fair market value of the asset ($200,000) by the annuity factor for a fifty-year-old (8.4743).

There are some disadvantages to this technique. Clearly, there are going to be some income tax ramifications; there will be capital gains and ordinary income to the seller. Furthermore, in order for this technique to work, the buyer's promise to repay the seller cannot be secured. Therefore, there is some risk to the seller that the buyer will not in fact make the annual payments, and if that happens, the seller is under some risk that the asset will not be able to be retrieved.

You can see that this technique would be exceedingly

useful for a seller who was not likely to live his actuarily determined life expectancy. Some sellers have, in fact, been aggressive with this technique, and have sold assets shortly before their death. The IRS takes the position that if the seller's death is "clearly imminent," this technique cannot be used. No one quite knows what "clearly imminent" means, and in fact sellers who have had serious types of cancer or other life-threatening diseases have managed to successfully use this technique.

Self-canceling Installment Note

This technique is very similar to the private annuity. The idea is that an asset is sold for its fair market value to a buyer, usually a family member, who then promises to pay the seller in installments. The hope is that the seller will die before all the installments are repaid; the technique will then authorize and allow the cancelation of the unpaid installments. In this way, a valuable asset can be transferred to a member of the family with very little money being repaid and only a small amount included in the seller's taxable estate.

The self-canceling installment note differs from the private annuity in that in the former technique, the buyer agrees to pay the seller in fixed annual installments over a fixed number of years; in the latter technique, the annual installments are likewise fixed but will run until the seller dies, whenever that may be. In other words, with the self-canceling installment note, the buyer knows exactly the maximum number of years he or she will have to make the annual installment payments. Those number of years cannot exceed the seller's life expectancy. If the seller should die before the entire balance is paid back to him, the unpaid balance will be canceled, and will not count as part of the seller's taxable estate.

EXAMPLE: A father sells his $1 million farm to his son. Using actuarial tables, the father's life expectancy is found to be twenty years. The son agrees to pay the father the $1 million in nineteen equal annual installments. The promissory note, which the son signs, includes a provision that says that if the father dies before the nineteen installments are completely paid off, the balance will be canceled and will not form a part of father's taxable estate. The father dies three years after his son signs the note. The son will therefore have bought a $1 million asset for $3/19$ of its value. The balance, $16/19$, will not be included in the father's taxable estate, and will "vanish" from the tax system.

As you might suspect, both the private annuity and the self-canceling installment note are tricky. The IRS has these things in its sights, and probably won't accept them without a fight. So before you set one up, see your lawyer.

Charitable Gifts

Any amount you leave to an IRS-qualified charity is completely free of estate tax, and counts as a deduction against your taxable estate.

EXAMPLE: A mother and father have an estate of $3 million. They have both set up bypass trusts, which, as we know, can shelter $1.2 million of wealth from estate taxes. However, the balance of their estate, $1.8 million, will be fully taxed if it is left to a noncharitable beneficiary. If the parents leave all of this $1.8 million, or any part of it, to a charity, then the part that the charity receives will be tax-free. If, for example, they leave $1 million to a qualified charity, then only $800,000 of their estate would be subject to estate taxes. The catch with charitable giving is that while your estate gets an estate tax deduction for any amount going to a qualified charity, which is good, the kids or your other beneficiaries won't get the money, which may not be what you want.

Is there any method by which your estate can get a charitable deduction, you can leave some money to charity, and some money to your children (or other beneficiaries)? The answer is yes—you *can* do all three things and *with the same money*. The way this works is by setting aside a certain amount of money (or other assets) in a trust. The trust can take effect after you (and your spouse if you have a spouse) have both died. The trust would give a certain dollar or percentage amount to a charity for a certain number of years, and after those years are up, then the trust would distribute its principal to your children. Or you can do the reverse: The trust could give its income to your child or children or other beneficiaries for a set number of years (or until they die), and then at that point the trust principal would be distributed to the charity. In other words, the charity can get the money first, or second. The charitable deduction for your estate would depend upon how much income the charity gets, at what point in time it gets it, and for how long it gets it.

EXAMPLE: Sally Single has an estate of $1.1 million. She knows she can distribute the first $600,000 to her favorite nephew free of estate tax. However, the balance of her estate, $500,000 will be taxable unless Sally uses an estate reduction technique. Sally is charitable, but she doesn't want to give the entire amount to charity. Instead, getting assistance from her attorney with the appropriate IRS tables, she sets up a trust that will take effect when she dies and that will hold the $500,000. The trust is required to pay a recognized charity $56,650 each year for the next twenty years. At the end of the twenty year period, the trust principal and income then remaining will be distributed to Sally's nephew. The estate tax charitable deduction that Sally's estate will receive is equal to $500,000. Therefore, Sally's estate will pay no federal estate taxes.

Had she desired, Sally could have reduced the term of the trust from twenty years to a shorter period, or she could have reduced the annual amount going to charity from $56,650 to some smaller amount. If she does either of those things, or both of them, her charitable deduction for her estate will be smaller.

These kinds of trusts, which provide benefits both to charity and also to individual people, not only have estate tax benefits, but also can be structured to provide income tax benefits to you right now, while you're alive. Another very nice thing about charitable giving is that you may not even have to pay a lawyer to help you! You can simply go to your favorite charity, speak to them, and they can assist you for free.

Had Enough, or Do You Want More?

In the preceding pages, we've spoken about a few of the estate tax reduction techniques that you can utilize and which will serve to reduce your estate down to the $600,000 level (if you're single) or to the $1.2 million level (if you're married and use bypass trusts). There are other techniques as well: limited freeze family partnerships; corporate recapitalizations; grantor income trusts; generation-skipping trusts; and the list goes on. These techniques are even more exotic than the ones explained above.

It really comes down to this. Probate and estate taxes are voluntary. If you don't want to pay them, you can structure your estate and affairs in such a way so that you don't have to pay them. Many of the richest American families have managed to pass millions upon millions of dollars from generation to generation, with only negligible estate taxes. And much of this was done when estate tax rates were as high as 77 percent. But with a little planning and a little foresight, these familes managed to avoid the probate and tax system almost entirely.

Forget about the "inevitability" of death and taxes; start thinking about death and tax *avoidance*. The means are available. This book has given you a brief introduction to some of the techniques now popular in avoiding probate and estate taxes. The next step is up to you. Get motivated, and go see an expert for help.

About the Author

DAVID C. LARSEN studied law at the University of California at Los Angeles, where he was editor in chief of the *UCLA-Alaska Law Review*. Since 1975 he has lectured widely on the subjects of wills, probate, and inheritance taxes, including four guest appearances on "Good Morning, America." Mr. Larsen lives with his wife and daughter in Honolulu, where he is an attorney specializing in wills, trusts, and estate planning.